I0070706

Becoming The Leader Within

Built on Awareness, Conscientiousness, & the Willingness to Evolve

A. Harvey

ISBN: 979-8-218-66834-1
ISBN: 979-8-218-66835-8

Disclaimer

Throughout this book, I reference specific companies where I've had the privilege to work or engage professionally. Any mention of these organizations is solely for the purpose of providing context and clarity to the personal experiences, lessons, and leadership insights shared in this book.

My intent in using the names of these companies is not to speak on their behalf, disclose proprietary information, or represent their internal views, operations, or leadership practices. Instead, references are made purely to illustrate the environments and moments in which I learned, grew, and developed my own understanding of leadership.

I hold each company mentioned in the highest regard and am deeply appreciative of the opportunities, experiences, and mentorship I received during my time with them. Their influence helped shape my career and the perspectives I share here. This book reflects my personal journey and views alone and should not be interpreted as an official account or endorsement by any organization referenced.

Table of Contents

Introduction
How This Book is Structured

This book is built around a simple but powerful idea: leadership starts with paying attention. Not just to your title or your goals, but to your experiences, every one of them. The philosophy of ACE Leadership is rooted in three key principles: Awareness, Conscientiousness, and Evolve. Each principle forms a chapter of this book, and within each are focused, story-driven sections drawn from real moments and practical takeaways from my own leadership journey.

Awareness is about tuning in, to people, to your environment, and to yourself. It's the foundation of communication, trust, and emotional presence. Conscientiousness is about effort and follow-through, working hard, doing the right thing even when no one's watching, and owning your outcomes. And Evolve is where growth lives. It's about adapting with intention, learning from mistakes, and building strategies that move you, and others, forward.

Each reflection and lesson shared here is grounded in experience, not theory. Across a career that spans global organizations like Ericsson, Cadbury Schweppes, JCPenney, Santander, IBM, and others, I've had the opportunity to learn from incredible leaders, diverse teams, and real-world challenges. From entry level positions to executive roles, I've gained and applied lessons that shaped how I lead, and how I continue to grow. Whether you're leading others or simply learning to lead yourself, these stories are here to guide you forward, one moment at a time.

Throughout my career, I've placed a strong emphasis on developing my technical knowledge, continually educating myself, earning certifications, and staying close to the systems, processes, and tools that drive IT forward. That technical foundation has served me well, but this book isn't about being the most technical person in the room. And I'm not, and I don't strive to be. It's about leadership. It's about the power of collaboration, the strength of relationships, and the impact of enabling others. What I've learned, and continue to learn, is that real leadership doesn't come from having all the answers. It comes from knowing how to bring out the best in the people around you and giving others room to grow. That's where the work truly matters. That's when leadership becomes lasting.

Where it All Started for Me

My first paycheck came at age twelve, even though I had to say I was thirteen to get the job. I landed a paper route with the *Orange County Register*, a job that, in hindsight, shaped far more than my weekends. I wasn't chasing leadership lessons; I just wanted some spending money and a reason to ride my bike. But those early mornings, the heavy Sunday editions, and the persistent customers taught me something I didn't have the language for back then, showing up matters.

Those weren't strategic leadership lessons at the time. They were just life. But over time, I came to realize that even those moments were shaping how I approached responsibility, relationships, and resilience. I wasn't managing teams yet, but I was already learning how to lead myself.

From there, I took every job I could. Mowing lawns, shoveling dirt, hauling hay. I didn't ask what the pay was, I just said yes. That willingness to show up, to do the work others avoided, became my edge. And without knowing it, I was developing the foundation that would support me through future roles in operations, IT, and ultimately, leadership.

This book is built from those experiences, from delivering newspapers to eventually leading cyber security programs and executive teams at global enterprises. The jobs changed. The stakes got higher. But the principles stayed the same: pay attention, work hard, keep growing.

I didn't set out to become a leader. I just learned to notice the opportunities in front of me, to adapt when I failed, and to keep showing up. Somewhere along the way, I discovered that leadership isn't about titles, it's about how you carry yourself when no one's watching.

Here's the premise: leadership is learned, and it often starts earlier than you think. You don't need to have all the answers. You just need to stop running on autopilot and start paying attention.

Introduction To Awareness

Awareness is the foundation of effective leadership. It's not just about being present, but being deeply in tune with your people, your environment, and the small details that often go unnoticed. In this section, we explore how everything matters, from the way you communicate to the moments you choose to step in or step back. You'll see how trust and credibility are built, or lost, through consistent action, and why every message you deliver whether spoken or silent carries lasting weight. We also dive into situational awareness, the ability to read the room and adjust with intention. Mistakes will happen, but awareness helps you own them, learn from them, and lead forward. Together, these lessons form the core of leadership that is sharp, responsive, and real.

I once heard a story about a baseball coach who was struggling with the second baseman's lack of effort. Instead of confronting him directly, the coach tried something different. He pulled the player aside and said, "I'm having a hard time getting our first baseman to hustle to the bag. Next time you have a play at first, fire the throw to first like you're trying to beat him there, even if he's not on the base yet." The second baseman nodded, took the challenge, and suddenly started making sharper, quicker plays. What he didn't realize was that the coach's message wasn't really about the first baseman at all, it was about him. The coach knew that giving him ownership and purpose would elevate his game. It worked. The infield tightened up, the tone changed, and the second baseman became more engaged. It was a quiet lesson in how thoughtful leadership can course correct without confrontation but by shifting perspective and inspiring self-driven accountability.

For longer than I care to admit, I wasn't aware of much beyond the task in front of me. I came in, did the work, and left, day after day. I didn't know who the senior leaders were. I couldn't tell you what other teams did, or even why it mattered. My world was narrow by choice, not because the opportunity wasn't there, but because I didn't know how to look for it.

I began my technical career at a global telecommunications company called Ericsson. It was a name known around the world, filled with some of the brightest technical minds in the industry delivering world-class telecommunications solutions. And yet, I was in the least technical role on the team. I delivered computers to employees, set them up, and made sure everything powered on. That was my job, and I focused on doing it well.

In hindsight, I realized I was surrounded by individuals who could have had a meaningful impact on my career had I taken the initiative to engage more intentionally. I worked alongside engineers, architects, and leaders with deep technical expertise and valuable perspectives, but I remained narrowly focused on my day-to-day tasks. I missed opportunities to connect, to ask questions, and to broaden my understanding of the organization and its people.

Still, my time at the company was both formative and rewarding. Before moving on to a new opportunity at another technical organization, I had the chance to rotate through several teams, including Help Desk, Site Support, Server Support, Network, and ultimately, the Email team. While I gained a significant amount of technical knowledge, I lacked the awareness to recognize the leadership opportunities around me. I didn't yet understand the importance of being present in the moment or how those early interactions could shape my development as a contributor and, eventually, as a leader.

Some of my fondest professional memories stem from my time at that company. I was early in my career during the Y2K transition and part of the overnight watch team, ready to respond should anything go wrong. As it turned out, the crisis never came, and I fell asleep on one of those quiet shifts, an amusing reminder of how much concern surrounded an event that proved largely uneventful. Beyond that, the role provided opportunities I never imagined. I had the chance to travel internationally, experience different cultures firsthand, and expand my perspective far beyond the walls of the office. Many of the relationships I formed during that time have endured, becoming both meaningful connections and lasting professional alliances that continue to add value even today.

It wasn't until I moved on to my next role that the lessons from my time at Ericsson began to take root. They sank in later than I would have liked but that's the nature of growth. Sometimes, we only recognize the significance of certain moments in retrospect. The important thing is that we do reflect and use those reflections to move forward with greater clarity and intention. This was the place where I received my first major break in the corporate world, and for that, I am sincerely grateful. To everyone who invested their time, guidance, or support, no matter how big or small, I want to extend a heartfelt thank you. Your contributions helped shape my early career, often in ways I didn't fully understand at the time. As I reflect on that chapter now, I recognize just how meaningful it was. It laid the groundwork for the leader I would eventually become, and I will always look back on the experience as a defining and valued part of my journey.

This section is personal to me because awareness didn't come naturally. It had to be earned through mistakes, reflection, and a growing curiosity about the world around me. If I had understood sooner that leadership begins with observation, perhaps I would have stepped into it earlier. But I'm grateful for the lessons, and in sharing them, I hope you'll spot your own moments sooner than I did.

All In From The Start

From Action to Awareness

The story of how my professional career began isn't just a memory, it's the groundwork for how I've come to view leadership. That first job didn't teach me everything I needed to know, but it taught me everything I needed to become someone who was ready to learn. I didn't show up to that interview with qualifications, I showed up with conviction. And while I was wildly under qualified on paper, I was fully committed in mindset. That one decision to go all in shifted the trajectory of my career. It taught me that effort, curiosity, and belief in yourself are sometimes more valuable than the resume you bring to the table.

As I grew in my role, what I started to recognize is that leadership isn't built in a single moment. It's built in how you respond to all the little ones. Every new experience, every problem solved, every uncomfortable stretch started to teach me not just how to work harder, but how to think differently. I moved from taking instruction to asking better questions. I stopped just trying to do the right thing and began trying to understand why it was right in the first place. And that's when things really began to shift. Growth wasn't just about showing up anymore it was about being present, being thoughtful, and paying attention to what was happening around me and within me.

That transition from doing to thinking is where leadership starts to deepen. This next section is about that exact shift. It's about building awareness, not just of your surroundings, but of your own perspective. It's about understanding the unconscious forces, like cognitive biases, that shape the decisions we make without us even realizing it. The more you understand your own mind, the more intentional you can be in how you lead. You don't have to be perfect to be a great leader, but you do have to be aware. Let's start there.

Failed Interview to Career Beginnings

My first corporate job interview was a complete disaster. I was interviewing for an entry level IT role at Ericsson, who had a presence in Texas. I lived in Arkansas, and I was desperate for an opportunity to break into something bigger. It should have been a slam dunk. I was recommended by my mom, who worked there and knew the hiring manager. But there was one big problem. I didn't know IT. Not at all.

Within minutes of the phone interview, it was painfully clear I was out of my depth. What should have been a formality turned into a reality check. I was unprepared, embarrassed, and out of my league. When they invited me for a follow up in person interview, I still didn't have the skills, but I had a mindset. I said yes with everything I had. I told them I was willing to quit my job, move states, and give it everything. "If I don't work out, fire me", I said, and I meant it. And they hired me. That moment defined the start of my IT career and my belief that if you go all in on yourself, others will too.

From that point forward, I committed fully to learning and growth. I raised my hand for every opportunity, enrolled in courses, earned certifications, and made it a priority to support others wherever I could. At the time, I didn't fully realize it, but I wasn't just building skills, I was building value. I was becoming someone others could rely on, someone who delivered. That level of commitment came with trade-offs. I sacrificed time with family, distanced myself from friends, and often pushed my own well-being aside. Looking back, I may have gone all in too hard, too fast, but at the time, I felt I had to. I was determined to build a long-term career in IT, and I had put too much on the line to let it slip away. Conviction requires sacrifice, and I was fully invested.

Years later, I left that company as a Messaging Manager, having advanced through roles in help desk, infrastructure, and team leadership. The experiences I gained during that time laid the foundation for the leader I am today, grounded in effort, sharpened by challenge, and shaped by the lessons I earned along the way. At times, I wasn't supposed to be there, at least that's how it felt. But I earned my spot by working harder, staying curious, and never waiting for someone else to move me forward. This mindset isn't just about career growth, it's about how you show up every day. It's about being the best version of yourself, even when you're tired, stuck, or unsure. Hard work matters. Showing up matters. Believing in yourself matters. And if you can do those things consistently, you'll start to realize that the snowball only grows when you give it the first push.

And along the way, yes, people will give you advice. Listen to all of it. Take in what fits, discard what doesn't. But most importantly, keep learning. Understand your own biases and how they can shape your decisions. Growth isn't about being perfect, it's about being aware. My story started with a lie about knowing IT. But the truth I found in the process, that's what changed everything.

From Doing to Thinking

Starting out in my career, success was defined by action. Show up early, work hard, say yes often, and stay curious. And for a long time, that worked. It helped me earn trust, gain experience, and create opportunities where none existed. I was moving forward by doing. But eventually, I realized that doing alone isn't enough to lead well. As your responsibilities grow, the way you think starts to matter more than how much you can get done in a day. Leadership becomes less about being the one who solves everything and more about how you approach the problem to begin with.

That's when I started shifting from just doing the work to thinking about how and why I was doing it. I began to notice patterns in behavior, both mine and others. I paid closer attention to decisions, to reactions, to the way conversations unfolded. I realized that so many of our choices at work aren't just about logic or facts, they're shaped by what we think we know, what we assume to be true, and what we believe without question. That's where the real evolution started for me.

The next section of this book dives into the part of leadership that most people don't talk about enough, which is how you think. It's about awareness, perception, and understanding the hidden forces that shape our judgment. It's about cognitive biases and how they influence your decisions, your relationships, and even the culture you help build. Because once you start to understand the way you think, you begin to lead with greater clarity, intention, and impact.

A Brief Overview of Biases

Cognitive Biases

Cognitive biases are systematic errors in thinking that influence the decisions and judgments we make. They arise from our brain's attempt to simplify complex information, often leading to distorted perceptions, irrational behavior, or flawed conclusions. While these biases are a normal part of how we process the world and can help us make quick decisions, they can also result in mistakes, particularly in emotional or high stakes situations. For example, confirmation bias leads us to favor information that supports our existing beliefs, while anchoring bias causes us to rely too heavily on the first piece of information we encounter. Hindsight bias makes us believe, after the fact, that an outcome was predictable, even if it wasn't. Negativity bias pulls our attention more strongly to negative experiences than positive ones, and optimism bias leads us to believe we're less likely to experience negative events compared to others.

Social Biases

Social biases, on the other hand, are unconscious attitudes or stereotypes that shape our understanding, actions, and decisions about other people, often without us realizing it. These biases influence how we perceive and interact with others based on group membership such as race, gender, age, or social status. In group bias makes us favor those who belong to our group, while out group bias leads us to view those outside our group more negatively. Stereotyping causes us to assign traits to individuals based on assumptions about the group they belong to. The halo effect skews our judgment by assuming someone who is good at one thing is good at everything, while the horn effect does the opposite, one negative trait colors our perception of a person's overall character or competence.

Decision Making Biases

Decision making biases are another category that significantly affects how we evaluate choices and form strategies. These biases emerge from our brain's use of mental shortcuts to manage complex decisions, often at the cost of clarity and objectivity. The framing effect alters our perception based on how information is presented, even if the underlying facts remain the same. Loss aversion makes us more motivated to avoid losses than to achieve equivalent gains. The bandwagon effect pushes us to adopt beliefs or behaviors simply because others do, and status quo bias leads us to favor the current state of things, resisting change even when a better option exists. Recognizing these biases is a critical step in improving decision making and leading with greater awareness and fairness.

Train Yourself to Work Past Biases

Once you realize your thinking can be biased, the most powerful thing you can do is start watching for it. Biases are an invisible influence that sneak into your decisions without warning. You're not alone, everyone is vulnerable to them. But awareness is your defense. You won't always avoid them, but you'll start thinking more clearly when you know they're in play. The best way to challenge bias? Ask questions. Stick to facts. Stay curious. Keep digging until you truly understand what's in front of you.

I ask questions constantly. It's how I learn, how I uncover blind spots, and how I test ideas. Sometimes I even take a concept to the extreme just to see where it breaks. Try this, imagine going an entire day at work without asking a single question, not even "how was your weekend?" That might be manageable, but what about getting the latest budget figures? Confirming if something was completed on time? Verifying a system update? You'd be stuck.

The truth is, you can't lead or grow without asking questions. Unless you plan to do every task yourself, which isn't realistic, the questions are how you move work forward. So be curious. Be relentless. Ask until you understand. That's not just how you lead, it's how you think smarter. Questions for me are the key to breaking down the influence of biased thinking.

Lessons Learned

The story in this chapter isn't just about how a career began, it's a blueprint for how you can approach your own. If you've ever felt under qualified, unsure, or like you didn't belong, know this: belief in yourself can be a powerful starting point. You don't have to have all the answers to begin, but you do need to be willing to say yes, to show up fully, and to commit to the work ahead. The first step is rarely perfect. It's the step after the one where you decide to give everything you've got that defines the direction you'll go.

As you grow in your own journey, remember that leadership isn't built on titles or technical skills alone. It's built in the small, daily decisions to stay curious, to ask questions, and to push yourself beyond what's comfortable. Doing the work is important but learning how to think critically about the work is what turns effort into growth. Pay attention to what's happening around you and within you. Let each experience sharpen your awareness and deepen your understanding of what leadership really requires.

And as you continue, don't just rely on your instincts, challenge them. Understand that biases influence your thinking, even when you're unaware. Stay curious. Ask questions until you understand. Be someone who's always learning, always growing, and always ready for what's next. Because if you want to build a meaningful career, one that evolves with intention and impact, it starts with a choice to go all in, again and again.

Trust and Credibility

It Takes Time to Build, But Only a Moment to Lose

Trust isn't something you should ever have to ask for, especially at work. Either people trust you, or they don't. And while trust can absolutely be earned, it shouldn't be something you rely on without continuing to prove it. The most meaningful trust is built quietly, over time, often without you realizing it. You're just doing your job showing up, delivering, being reliable. Then one day a leader asks for a report, and you hand it over without hesitation. That moment, small as it seems, builds trust. And enough moments like that can open the door to bigger opportunities.

As a leader, when it's time to assign an important project, you don't want to guess, you want someone you can count on. Sometimes there's only one person who comes to mind. That doesn't mean the project is a given. Your job isn't to just hand out work. It's to ensure the right work gets done the right way and drives the right value for the business. If you don't trust that one person to deliver, you may not move forward at all. In those cases, you might still assign the work with clear coaching and support because they need a stretch goal. Or you may look beyond your immediate team if the right person isn't there. You may even split the work so two people grow together. That's leadership. Your job is to deliver value while helping others grow. That often means thinking creatively about how to get work done and who's ready to do it next.

The Foundation of Trust in Leadership

I learned a powerful lesson about leadership and trust, one I didn't expect to come from a friendly game of darts. My boss and I were on a business trip to Sweden, with a layover in New York. We grabbed dinner at a local pub, and over a few laughs and beers, made a lighthearted bet. The loser would carry the winner's luggage for the entire trip. Neither of us were dart champions, but we were both confident enough to shake on it. I ended up winning. And without hesitation, my boss honored the bet. He carried my luggage through airports, into hotels, and right past groups of our peers at a major event. It was awkward at times, but he never flinched. No excuses, no backpedaling, just follow through. That situation, simple as it was, left a lasting impression. He had my trust from then on, not because of the bet itself, but because he kept his word when it would've been easier not to.

In leadership, trust is built in moments like these not in grand gestures, but in quiet consistency. Whether you're helping a teammate, owning a task, or following through on a promise, your actions define your credibility. You never know who's watching or what moment will set the tone for your leadership. Keep your word. Do what you say you'll do. And when the moment comes, let others see that your integrity is something they can count on.

I learned that again in a very different way when I stepped into a new role under a new leader. This was during my time at JCPenney. After being given tasks, I'd often respond with "I got it," a phrase I'd used throughout my career to signal confidence and follow-through. What I didn't realize was that my predecessor had used those exact same words but consistently failed to deliver. So, when I said it, it landed wrong. I could feel my leader checking in more often, following up repeatedly, and I didn't understand why at first. It wasn't personal, it was history. I was working through a layer of unseen mistrust I hadn't created but still had to overcome. It wasn't until I asked a peer if they knew why. They explained, and then I understood. It taught me that trust doesn't always reset with a new title or new team. Sometimes, you must rebuild what someone else left behind not with words, but with action. Over time, trust was rebuilt. But it reminded me that consistency earns trust, and every interaction is either strengthening it or weakening it whether you see it or not. I also chose to continue to use that phrase to be consistent with not only my message and who I was. I could have elected to stop using it but decided to work through it so I could continue to be genuine to who I was and how I communicated commitment.

Trust Isn't an Entitlement

Trust is a leadership asset no matter what your title. Whether you're an individual contributor or leading a team, you're always building the trust that will carry you forward. Trust is earned through consistent actions, not charisma or confidence alone. Confidence helps open the door, but trust keeps you in the room. And while trust can take a long time to build, it can be lost in an instant. That's why it's so valuable and why it matters so much.

If you're stepping into a new leadership role, you may inherit trust you haven't yet earned. Some leaders have a presence that makes trust seem automatic, they connect easily, they communicate well, they lead with purpose. But it's rarely luck. More often, it's the result of years of showing up, doing the work, adding value, and building relationships. And when you lead, you don't just earn trust, you give it. The best teams are built on reciprocal trust. You must be willing to believe in others the way you want them to believe in you.

Now, I'll be the first to admit I've got my quirks. If you've worked with me, you probably know a few. I call out "pet peeve number twelve" when someone doesn't keep their calendar updated. I might toss in a sarcastic "thanks for showing up" if I pass your desk after a late arrival. It's all in good fun, but there's a point, consistency and professionalism matter. These little things, these habits, they add up. And over time, they become your brand, the things people trust you for.

So how do you build trust? Do the basics but do them well and do them consistently.

Keep your calendar updated. Follow through on what you say you'll do. Be on time. Be prepared. Communicate clearly. Help others when they need it. These may seem small, but they're the exact things people count on. Trust isn't built in big, dramatic moments, it's built in the daily detail. And when your team sees that they can count on you in those details, you won't have to ask for trust. You'll already have it.

A Short List of Daily Trust Building Habits

1. If you commit to a time-based task, deliver on time. If you can't, explain why
2. Communicate in a way that everyone understands the message
3. Listening is not waiting for your turn to talk, if you're listening, listen
4. If you make a mistake, admit it, then without being asked, fix it
5. Always be prepared
6. Recognize the efforts of others, say thank you
7. Be present, don't be that person who says "sorry, can you repeat that"
8. If you can say something in three words, don't use twenty.
9. Be honest, if you don't know you don't know, don't make things up
10. Show up to meetings on time, yours and others
11. End meetings on time, if you need more time, schedule a follow-up
12. Keep your calendar updated, it shows you can and do manage your time
13. Ask for help when you need it, don't ask for it if you don't, others know the difference
14. Offer help without being asked
15. Treat everyone with the same respect, even when they may not deserve it
16. Share and give credit to others, you can't do it alone, it does take a village
17. Say thank you

The above is not a comprehensive list by any means. You see, however, that all these are grounded in consistency, humility, and respect. Trust isn't built through grand gestures, it's earned through small, repeatable actions that demonstrate reliability, clarity, and integrity. These habits may seem simple, but they're often overlooked. Practicing them daily creates a culture of accountability and earns you credibility as a leader who not only talks about trust but lives it.

Let's take a moment to talk about number sixteen. There's more on this in a later chapter but it's worth focusing on now. If you're a leader, you can't do it alone. Collaboration isn't optional, it's the job. You need your team. You need partnerships. Almost nothing meaningful gets done in isolation. And if you're not yet a leader but aiming to be one, there's no better way to prove you're ready than by doing what leaders do, lead through others, and give credit where it's due.

Recognizing others for their contributions is one of the simplest and most powerful leadership moves you can make. First, because it's true, rarely does success come from a solo effort. And second, because when you call out others for the role they played, you're showing that you understand what leadership looks like. It's not about claiming the spotlight; it's about reflecting it.

If you're hoping to move into a leadership role, start here. Show that you can lead by recognizing the people around you. When your team wins, don't just say we did it, say *they* did it. Give credit publicly. Acknowledge people's impact. That's how you show you're not just focused on your own advancement, but on building others up too. And that's what leaders do. Recognition isn't a finishing touch; it's the closing loop in the leadership cycle. Without it, nothing feels complete. With it, trust grows, morale improves, and leadership becomes something others want to follow.

The Language of Trust

I want to talk about the language of trust in the workplace for a minute. The words you choose and the way you say them matter more than most people realize. If you're in a leadership role, your tone, timing, and honesty are part of how people decide whether to follow you. Trust is built not just on what you say, but how you say it. When you make promises, keep them. When you don't know something, admit it. The moment you start speaking in vague terms or dodging the truth, people recognize it even if they don't say anything. Leaders who speak plainly, with humility and clarity, tend to draw people in. The ones who speak with buzzwords, deflection, or corporate filler tend to create distance. I'm not a fan of acronyms for example. I do catch myself using them. Using acronyms without realizing it may leave some people behind. It also may portray you as knowing something others don't. If you must use them, make sure everyone knows what they mean and stand for, everyone.

What about metaphors. Use them but use them carefully. A well-placed metaphor can add levity or drive a point home with a touch of personality. If you lean on them too heavily, it starts to feel like you're dancing around your message. If every other sentence is a story about sailing the ship or taming the wild horse of workplace productivity, people might smile, but they'll still walk away unsure of what you actually meant. If you want to drive a point about looking into the details of an issue to solve an ongoing problem, say it. If you instead "look under the hood" too many times, your message will drift. As a leader, clarity is king. When you use metaphors, use them to lighten the moment or to add texture to an already clear message not to replace the message altogether. If people need to decode your words like a riddle, you're not building trust. You're building confusion.

One of the subtle ways leaders lose credibility is through the overuse of buzzwords and filler language that clouds their message. At one point, it seemed like everyone ended sentences with "right?" as if seeking validation for even the most straightforward points.

Lately, the word "hey" has crept into professional communication in strange ways: *"If we commit to this task, and they say hey, how are you going to do that?"* It's become a habit of asking yourself a question mid-sentence, turning clear statements into confusing monologues. Adding unnecessary noise will erode confidence. When leaders rely too heavily on these verbal crutches, their clarity suffers and with it, their credibility. Trust isn't built through jargon, metaphors, or manufactured emphasis. It's built through clear, direct, and intentional communication. Speak plainly. Say what you mean. When you do, people won't just hear you, they'll believe you.

And it's not just about what you say in the big meetings. The language of trust is built in passing moments like in hallway conversations, quick emails, and small check-ins. "I can help you with that" and "I'll take care of that" mean something but only when you follow through. The quickest way to erode trust is to over promise and under deliver. People remember how you made them feel, and your language matters, a lot.

Speak with intention. Be clear. Be real. That's how trust sounds.

Lessons Learned

Trust isn't something you ask for, it's something you earn, one small moment at a time. I've learned that it's not built through grand gestures or big projects, but through consistency, clarity, and keeping your word. Whether you're delivering a report without being asked, showing up prepared, or owning your mistakes and fixing them without excuses, each action quietly adds to your credibility. What I didn't fully understand early in my career is that trust is always being tested. You may not even know it's on the line, but people are watching how you speak, how you follow through, and how you treat others when no one's looking.

What I've also learned is that trust goes both ways. As a leader, you must give it if you expect to receive it. That means recognizing effort, sharing credit, and being real with your team. You can't fake it, and you can't shortcut it. Trust is earned through humility, transparency, and action. It's in the way you talk, the way you lead, and the way you show up even when it's inconvenient. The most respected leaders I've worked with weren't perfect, but they were consistent. They spoke clearly, followed through, and did what they said they would do. That's the kind of leader I strive to be. And the lesson is simple: Trust, once built, becomes your greatest leadership asset but you must work for it every single day.

Communicating Effectively

Speaking When it Matters Even if it's Hard

I'm not a great public speaker. I've known this for quite some time, and it's kept me away from several opportunities in my career. I occasionally find myself a part of a large project or a team being recognized and asked if I'd like to speak. In these moments, I usually defer to somebody else with more speaking prowess or charisma. These, for me, have always been nervous moments and missed opportunities.

Once, in front of an entire IT organization at an all-hands gathering at Kraft, I had the opportunity to represent my team's success during an event. Recalling this moment now, I can't remember exactly what I said, but from what I recall, it was a sentence or less. Something along the lines of teamwork, working hard, I really don't remember. I only remember being very nervous and not wanting to do it. There's something about everyone in an audience being completely quiet, focusing their entire attention on what you have to say. I attended a few courses that helped you with public speaking, and I just couldn't get through them. In my leadership tool chest, I would be lying to say that this tool isn't sharp. More truthfully, this tool isn't even in the toolbox at all.

Not only are these missed opportunities for me as a leader, but they're missed opportunities for me as a leader to recognize my team or individuals. What I've started to do late in my career is to sign up for more opportunities like this. I'll admit I don't sign up for the scary ones. I sign up for the ones that help me progressively get better at this. For example, I've recently started participating in panel discussions. In a panel discussion, I have others around me, which take the focus directly off me. In this type of format, my portion is also reduced in the amount of time I speak. I'm able to treat these moments like discussions rather than presentations. Having done a few of these and getting more comfortable, I'm convinced that one day I'll be able to stand up in front of a crowd and give a presentation without wanting to run and hide.

I share this to illustrate a point about communications. All kinds of communications that leaders use to deliver a message to a group or individuals via emails, instant messages, meetings, phone calls, and, of course, public speaking. Each of these mediums serve a purpose. As a leader, you should use every opportunity to get your message across. I'm not great at public speaking, so I've tried to hone my other skills in communication. If you're good at something, you should take advantage of that and continue to do it. A contradictory belief that if you're bad at something, you should get better at it. I believe that you should focus on both, but with a primary focus on the things you're good at. If you're a more effective communicator in email or in meetings, then use those opportunities to your advantage. Don't shy away from the areas you're not good at, though, because to be an effective leader, you must be able to communicate across multiple mediums to reach as many people as possible.

Email

I want to take a moment to talk about email because it's easy to overlook, but it's one of the most widely used forms of communication in business. As a leader, or someone aspiring to lead, how you write an email can carry just as much weight as what you say in person. It's not just about information. It's about tone, timing, and clarity. You're not there to explain your intent in real time, so the words must do all the work. That means thinking before you hit send. What's the goal of the message? Is the tone aligned with the situation? Are you being clear, or are you hiding behind long paragraphs and vague phrasing? I've made the mistake of misspelling someone's name, hitting send when I'm still composing, and the dreaded send to the wrong person or even worse, sending to a distribution list when intending to make a personal comment to smaller list of recipients. Take care in email. It's forever.

I share this because I've learned that how you say something in an email can either build trust or create confusion. A quick email asking for a status update can feel like micromanagement if it's rushed or abrupt. On the other hand, a short message expressing appreciation or encouragement can do more than a team meeting sometimes. The key is to know your audience. If you're emailing someone who's had a rough week, or you're delivering tough news, the message needs more care. The goal is always clarity and to connect. You want them to understand what you're saying, but also to feel that it was said with intention.

Before you send the email, pause and ask yourself one important question: *how will the reader interpret this?* Not how *you* feel writing it, not what *you* meant, but how it might land with the person on the other end. That's where leadership lives in the awareness of how your message will be received. It's easy to assume that your tone is obvious, or your intentions are clear, but email strips away body language, facial expressions, and even the warmth in your voice. That's why a sentence meant to be neutral can feel cold. Or a direct question can come across as aggressive. Take a moment to reread it from their perspective. Are you giving direction or sounding like you're doubting them? Are you asking for help or accidentally sounding demanding? That moment of reflection can be the difference between building trust and unintentionally eroding it.

I've also found that structure matters. Leading with the main point is a good start, especially if the reader is busy or overwhelmed. Then support it with context and always end with a clear next step or nothing at all if none is needed. Don't overcomplicate it. If your message requires more emotional intelligence than a written format can deliver, consider switching mediums. But if email is the best choice, take the time to read it out loud before sending it. That's how you hear your tone. That's how you stay aware of how it lands. Communication is a tool, and email is a big one so use it wisely.

Saying thank you at the end of an email with your name beside it is a nice touch as well.

Someone once told me that they don't like to say thank you at the end of an email because normally the person you're sending it to, didn't actually do anything for you. This may be an accurate statement, but it doesn't deliver the right tone. I tend to feel more comfortable in future conversations with the knowledge I've been appreciative.

Instant Messaging and Chat

Then there's instant messaging. It's quick, casual, and easy. But that ease is exactly why it can go wrong. Because when something's fast, we tend to think less about how we say it. Instant messaging is like the hallway conversation of the digital world, and it happens in real time, without much filter. That's why leaders must be intentional, even in chat. A short message can carry more weight than you think. A "Can we talk?" with no context can cause unnecessary stress. A missed "thanks" or "great job" can make your team feel like their effort went unnoticed. As with email, be careful and cautious before hitting send. In my opinion it's somehow easier to accidentally send the right message to the wrong person. When you work in email you tend to do it one at a time. When you send an instant message you routinely have several arriving at the same time. They're all just sitting there in a queue, pulling on your attention. Waiting.

I've learned that tone doesn't always carry well over chat. Humor, sarcasm, or even enthusiasm can get lost or misunderstood. That is without a myriad of various smiley faces. So clarity becomes even more important. Be brief, but not abrupt. Be clear, but not cold. I like to open with context. Just one sentence that frames the message and then gets to the point. And I always try to end with a human touch, even if it's as small as an emoji or a "let me know if you have questions". It may sound simple, but it goes a long way in showing people that you're not just firing off instructions, instead you're communicating with intention. Don't overuse emoji's though. Leaders are human, but they're also not children. There's a fine line in using emoji's, be tactical with their usage and it also might help to be up on the latest meaning with some of them. An emoji or two, maybe OK. More than two and your leadership erodes.

What makes instant messaging powerful is also what makes it risky. It's easy to reach people, but also easy to overwhelm them. So, timing matters. If it's not urgent, maybe it doesn't need to be sent at 8 PM. If it's feedback, maybe it's better delivered in person or in a more thoughtful format. The bottom line is this, being a leader doesn't mean sending more messages, it means sending the right ones, at the right time, in the right way. Instant messaging isn't just a convenience. It's a tool, and when used thoughtfully, it can help you lead with presence, even when you're not in the room.

When it comes to using instant messaging in team chats, there's a balance to strike. As a leader, you set the tone intentionally or not. Team channels aren't just for updates, they're a reflection of your team's culture. Use that space to model clear, respectful communication. Share wins publicly, give credit where it's due, and ask questions in a way that invites collaboration, not defensiveness. Avoid calling people out in front of others for mistakes, use private messages for that. And when you do post something to the group, make sure it's helpful, timely, and easy to understand. Overloading a chat with scattered thoughts or unclear requests only creates noise. But when you use that space to connect, inform, and lift others up, you turn a simple tool into something that builds alignment and trust.

An item to note, I'm very upfront and clear with my team about privacy and confidentiality. Everyone should be able to express themselves, be open and honest and not shy away from difficult conversations. I have a few rules, however that I am very strict to sticking to. What is said amongst the team, stays in the team, and we do not share anything that was discussed especially if it involves information that needs to remain private and confidential. I also expect everyone to remain professional and respect each other. We are all professionals, and at work to deliver on business outcomes. As we spend on average a third of our lives at work Monday through Friday it is completely acceptable to have a good laugh amongst the team. Just not at anyone's expense that makes them feel uncomfortable, unwanted, or not part of your team's culture.

Group and Team Meetings

Group meetings are one of those things that can either be incredibly useful or feel like a waste of time. It all depends on how you approach them. As a leader, how you run a meeting says a lot about how you lead. Are you prepared? Are you giving people a voice? Are you using that time to move things forward or just filling space on the calendar? I've found that the most effective team meetings are the ones where everyone leaves with more clarity than they had when they walked in. That doesn't happen by accident. You've got to have a purpose, an agenda, and a plan to stick to it. I've also learned that meetings aren't just about updates, they're about connection. It's one of the few times the team is all in the same place, mentally and physically, even if it's over voice or video. I like to make space for a little humanity. A quick check-in, a moment to recognize someone's effort, or even just a pause to let someone speak who doesn't usually jump in. Those small moments add up. They build trust. They show people that this isn't just a machine, it's a group of people working together toward something that matters. This isn't just for the team's sake; this is how I like to engage as well. Connecting with people shouldn't be a chore, it should be a gift.

And if you want your team to value the meeting, you must show them you value their time. That means starting on time, ending on time, and not letting the loudest voice dominate the room. It means knowing when to table a conversation and when to dig deeper. Leading a group meeting isn't about holding court, it's about facilitating a space where ideas, feedback, and alignment can happen. And when done well, it becomes a rhythm your team can rely on.

I once reported to a leader who told me that at the end of every meeting, he made sure he said something. If he had not said anything throughout the entire meeting this was his way of leaving an impression that he had been there and contributed. He was giving me advice at the time because he wanted to see me be more visible. I took away from that advice instead that I might as well go ahead and talk during the meeting rather than try to fake my way through it at the very end. If you find yourselves in meetings that you're not engaging in ask yourself if you need to be there or are you just not being engaging. You don't always have to talk but at some point, if you recognize that you never do ask yourself why.

One on One Meetings

This is one of the most powerful leadership tools you have and some of the most underused. A one on one isn't just a check in a box to tick off. It's a space for real connection, real conversation, and real growth. It's one of the few times where your job is to listen more than talk. I've found that if you come in with an open mind and a good question, something like "What's been on your mind lately?" you'll learn more than you ever could from a status report. People want to be heard. They want to know that their voice matters beyond tasks and deadlines. I learned from a leader I look up to, to focus on three things, how are you, how's it going, and how can I help.

That's why consistency matters. Canceling or rescheduling a one on one all the time sends a message, whether you mean it or not that their time isn't as important as yours. But when you show up, prepared, and present, you create a space where trust can build week by week. I like to take notes not just on the work, but on the person. Goals, frustrations, wins. Then I follow up on those things later. It shows that I was paying attention. That I care about more than just productivity, I care about their growth.

The best one on ones don't just review what happened. They explore what's possible. Where does this person want to grow? What's getting in their way? How can you help them succeed? That's where leadership really shows up not in managing their time, but in investing in their future. And if you can create a space where people feel safe to be honest, you'll learn more than you expect, and you'll lead better because of it.

Lessons Learned

I've learned that communication is one of the most important tools in leadership not just delivering a message, but making sure it's understood. It took me time to realize that saying something once isn't enough. People don't always hear it the first time, and even if they do, they may not fully grasp it in the way you intended. I used to shy away from public speaking, passing up moments where I could have reinforced my message and recognized my team. But over time, I found other ways to build my voice through writing, through one on ones, through small conversations that, when repeated with consistency, created clarity. What I've come to understand is that leadership communication is about reinforcement, not repetition. You don't have to say it louder you have to say it better, and in the way that people can receive it.

Regardless of the method, email, chat, meetings, or hallway conversations, what matters is the intention behind the message. I've learned to pause, to consider how a message might land, and to choose clarity over complexity. Communication isn't just about delivering updates it's about building trust. The more mindful I became about tone, timing, and tailoring the message to the medium, the stronger my leadership became. And now I carry this mindset into every interaction: Say what matters, say it with purpose, and keep saying it until everyone's moving in the same direction. That's how leaders get heard not just in the moment, but in the momentum that follows.

The Weight of Words

Let's eat, Grandma. You may have seen this one before. This simple communication with your grandma informing her you both should eat now. Remove the comma and the message changes significantly. Your words matter. The way you say them matters even more. Continuing off the last chapter on communications, every message you send, whether it's in an email, a quick chat, or something you say in passing during a meeting, carries more weight than you think. As a leader, your words aren't just words, they're signals. They set the tone. They shape culture. They influence how people feel about their work, about themselves, and about you. I've learned that the tone isn't just about what's said out loud. It lives in punctuation, in timing, in how clearly you express yourself, and in how carefully you respond. That's why it's not enough to just get your point across, you must consider how it's going to land. Because when you lead, every message matters.

Language isn't just functional, it's directional. As a leader, people don't just listen to what you say; they interpret it. They fill in gaps. They react not just to the message itself, but to the feeling behind it. That's why leadership language must be deliberate. It's not about using bigger words or sounding polished. It's about being intentional. The same sentence, with a slight change in tone or timing, can encourage someone or shut them down. Words carry power. They can declare a tense moment, spark action, or quietly erode trust if not chosen carefully.

I've learned that people remember what leaders say in ways leaders often forget. A quick phrase in a meeting, a sentence at the end of an email, even a silence where a response was expected, all of it gets stored and replayed. When you're in a position of influence, your words become part of other people's inner dialog. That's a big responsibility. So, when you speak, ask yourself, am I being clear? Am I being thoughtful? Am I lifting someone up, or leaving them unsure? Because whether you meant it or not, the message is already being received. And that's the real work of leadership choosing language that aligns with your values, your vision, and the people you lead.

Always read your message from the recipient's perspective. Regardless of the media, email, Instant Message, in person, etc., think how it's being received. Put yourself in the same situation as the receiver, did you understand the message, deliverable, context, or whatever it was you were trying to get across.

Example

Let's use the following example: "I need a report of all clients that have opened requests". This request seems straightforward but how was this request received.

On the surface, it seems like a simple, clear request. But leadership communication isn't just about clarity, it's also about delivery. How was that request received? Was it seen as urgent? Demanding? Frustrated? Supportive? Motivated? The words are neutral, but the tone behind them matters. If the message came out of nowhere with no context, it might feel abrupt or even critical. A more effective approach might sound like, "When you get a chance today, could you run a report of all clients with open requests? It'll help us prioritize our response efforts." Same request, different tone and likely a very different reaction. By asking in this matter, you also inspire feedback and collaboration. The person running the report may have ideas on how you can improve your data review by adding additional fields or formatting. Ensuring others understand your message, and feel included you will build stronger trust, foster clearer collaboration, and create a culture where people feel seen, heard, and motivated to contribute. Leadership means thinking not just about what you say, but how it lands, and making sure your language encourages cooperation, not confusion or hesitation.

Communication is a two-way street, and clarity isn't solely the responsibility of the sender. The receiver also plays a critical role. If a message is unclear, vague, or lacks direction, it's up to the recipient to seek clarity. That means asking questions like: What does success look like? When is this needed? What specifically should be included? What are we trying to learn from this? These clarifying questions don't just improve the quality of the outcome, they show initiative, accountability, and a shared commitment to getting things right. Too often, breakdowns in communication are chalked up to "bad instructions," when neither side paused to confirm alignment. Effective teams make a habit of checking for understanding, not just assuming it. In leadership, it's not enough to hope your message landed. You must ensure it did, and as a recipient, you must make sure you receive it the way it was intended. That mutual responsibility is what builds trust, improves results, and keeps teams moving forward with purpose.

The Words Matter

I've found that some of the most effective leadership doesn't come from big speeches, it comes from small, intentional words used every day. Words like "thank you," "I appreciate that," "what do you think?" and "how can I help?" seem simple, but they carry a significant amount of weight. They show your team that you notice effort, that you value input, and that you're here to support not just to direct. Saying "great work" might take two seconds, but it reinforces a standard and encourages momentum. Even starting a sentence with "I just want to acknowledge…" can shift the tone of a conversation and create a moment of respect that lingers long after the words are said.

Respectful leadership also means choosing words that create space for others. Phrases like "I'd love your perspective," or "let's dig into your idea a bit more," turn conversations into collaboration. Instead of saying "you didn't do this," try "let's look at what might have gone wrong and how we can fix it." It's not about softening the truth it's about delivering it in a way that keeps people engaged and open. The best leaders know their words have impact, and they use that impact to build people up, create clarity, and move the team forward with intention and trust.

This reflection for me really reinforces how important it is to be consistent with your words. People remember how you talk to them, how you respond under pressure, and how you carry yourself when things are going well or when they aren't. I didn't realize it at the time, but the way I communicated day in and day out was quietly building a reputation. Saying "thank you," asking how I could help, giving credit where it was due those small things added up. I wasn't trying to build influence. I was just trying to be someone people wanted to work with. What I didn't realize was that consistency in how I spoke and carried myself was building trust, even when I wasn't paying attention to it. I often notice I say "thank you" when talking to Alexa. It's a habit at this point and comical but I'm OK with all of that. At least I'm consistent.

Over time, people began to seek out my opinion, invite me into projects, and ask for my input not because I was the loudest in the room, but because they saw me as someone who respected the team, and contributed with purpose. That didn't happen overnight. It came from repeating the small, respectful behaviors repeatedly until they became part of how people saw me. The consistency in my words created clarity. What I thought were just good habits turned out to be leadership in its most honest form. And looking back, I see now that the way you communicate, especially when no one's watching, is what shapes how others choose to follow you.

How Lack of Words Matter

Something that took me a while to truly understand is that listening is just as much a part of communication as speaking. As a leader it's easy to fall into the habit of asking questions just to check a box or move a conversation along. I used to ask a question, already thinking about the next task or what I was going to say next. But the moment I really started listening I noticed the difference. People could feel it. They open up more. They gave me better insights. They trusted me more. I wasn't just leading the conversation anymore. I was making space for someone else to lead a part of it too.

When you ask someone a question, especially as a leader, you owe it to them to hear the answer. That's not just about nodding along or waiting for a pause so you can jump back in. It means pausing, listening, and sometimes asking a follow-up question just to make sure you understood it right. I've found that repeating back what I heard, even in my own words, lets the other person know I was paying attention. And that kind of moment, where someone feels heard and seen, goes a long way. Listening shows people that their voice matters, and when you do it consistently, they'll bring you more honesty, more ideas, and more of themselves.

I didn't always see listening as a leadership skill, but now I think it's one of the most important ones. Because if you're not listening, you're not really communicating, you're just broadcasting. And leadership isn't about broadcasting your own thoughts all the time. It's about connections. It's about learning what your team needs, what they're thinking, and what they're not saying out loud. You get that through listening. It's quiet work, but powerful work. And the more you do it, the more you'll realize just how much you can lead without saying anything at all.

Don't just ask questions for the sake of asking them either. Make sure that you're asking questions that need answers and that others can contribute to. If you ask non-relevant questions for the sake of asking a question people will notice. As a leader your questions need to be thought out carefully. The questions you ask should direct business, guide goals, and further along objectives.

I'm inquisitive by nature and always feel like I have at least one more question to ask. In my home office I have a framed portrait of Albert Einstein. There's a caption at the bottom that reads "I have no special talents. I am only passionately curious." This quote by him highlights the importance he puts on curiosity and his thirst for knowledge. Questions to me are significant because by asking them you and others recognize that you don't have the answer and need it. Asking questions is collaborative and provides recognition that you trust others for the answer. Leadership isn't about always knowing, it's about always learning.

A dangerous gap in communication is the one left by silence. When we don't ask questions, when we assume instead of clarifying, we create space for misunderstanding, misalignment, and missed opportunities. I've seen it firsthand, projects derail, relationships strain, and trust erodes not because someone said the wrong thing, but because no one said anything at all. There's an old saying: "Don't let silence be your voice, let your voice be your voice." As leaders, we can't rely on silence to stand in for understanding. If something doesn't make sense, ask. If expectations aren't clear, clarify. If direction is missing, speak up. Because silence doesn't protect us, it isolates us. And in leadership, your voice is one of your most important tools. Use it with intention. Use it to connect. Use it to learn. But above all, use it.

A Final Word on Silence

I personally struggle with both being silent and being in silence at work. I incorrectly have the assumption that silence means nothing is happening and time is being wasted. I go into 'why am I here' and 'I could be doing something else' mode. This is something I actively work on being better at. Living through the awkwardness that is silence in a meeting can be very uncomfortable. People need time to think before speaking and sometimes that's just what silence is. We want people to think before they speak, right? Be sure to give silence a chance to turn into something meaningful. That's what I've had to remind myself. Silence isn't a void, it's a pause, and sometimes that pause is exactly where clarity begins. I've learned that if you rush to fill the silence, you might be cutting off the moment someone else was about to step into. Not everyone processes information at the same speed. Some people need a beat to collect their thoughts, to find the words, or to build the courage to speak up. And if you're always the first to jump in, you might never hear what they would've added. Giving silence a little space gives people permission to contribute at their own pace, not just yours.

What I've started doing is sitting in that discomfort a little longer. Letting the silence breathe instead of jumping over it. It's not easy, especially when you're used to leading with action, but leadership also means knowing when to hold space, not just fill it. And often, something valuable comes out of that silence, an idea, a question, a moment of honesty. It took time for me to trust that silence could be productive. But now I see it as part of the conversation, not a break from it. And that small shift has made a big difference in how I listen, how I lead, and how I connect with the people around me.

As a leader you're helping others grow themselves and by sitting in just the right amount of silence you're allowing others to use their voice.

Lessons Learned

I've come to realize that in leadership, your words aren't just words, they're signals. They set the tone, influence how people feel, and leave a lasting impression far beyond the moment. Whether it's a quick email, a meeting comment, or a passing remark, the way you speak carries more weight than you might think. I used to believe that saying the right thing once was enough. But I've learned that people don't just hear what you say they interpret it, remember it, and often replay it in their heads long after you've moved on. That's why intentional communication is so important. It's not about being polished, it's about being clear, thoughtful, and consistent in a way that makes people feel heard, respected, and understood.

What this chapter reinforces is that leadership communication lives in small details like saying thank you, choosing your words with care, asking thoughtful questions, and knowing when to speak and when to listen. Sometimes, the most powerful part of leadership is the silence you allow so others can step forward. Other times, it's the follow-through after a simple "I've got it" that builds trust. Words can lift people up, give them clarity, and create connection but only when they're spoken with intention. Over time, I've found that how I speak becomes how I'm known. And what I once thought were just habits, pausing before sending an email, rephrasing a message for clarity, listening more than I speak, turned out to be the very behaviors that shaped how others chose to follow me. Every message matter, especially when you don't think it does.

And perhaps the most important lesson of all: *don't let silence speak for you.* I've learned that unspoken thoughts often lead to unspoken expectations, and those turn into unmet outcomes. As leaders, we can't assume people know what we're thinking, what we expect, or how we feel. When something needs to be said, say it. When something is unclear, ask. Let your voice be your voice. Because while silence has its place, it should never replace your presence, your clarity, or your leadership. The people around you aren't just listening for your direction, they're looking for the reassurance that you're engaged, that you care, and that you're willing to communicate when it matters most.

Situational Awareness

From Peer to Manager

Situational awareness is one of those things I didn't fully appreciate until I became a leader in title. I was manager of a team for the first time, and it was for me a big deal. This highlighted that things had changed when I became a manager not in responsibility but in how others saw me in that role. Calling myself a leader at this point is a stretch, I was a manager who didn't understand leadership.

The scenario is a common one. The current manager position became available, and I applied for the role. Because I worked hard and had been in the team the longest, they promoted me. No management or leadership experience required, but the willingness to learn management. The company did send me to leadership training when the next course started. It was a new manager course that highlighted just the situation I had found myself in. Too bad I did not have the ability to attend prior to my first day. I do though believe that I learned more in this instance in how it played out. So here I was, the same people, same team, just me as the new manager. I dove straight in on being the new manager of the team. On day one I stayed later than normal thinking I needed to be the last person to leave. But as the time passed, I wondered why everyone was still at work. Turns out they had already left. I must have missed them. The next day the same thing happened but this time I realized what was happening. The normal route that everyone took to leave our area had been replaced by a longer route that avoided where I sat. They didn't want me to see when they left. Looking back now on that situation it strikes me that I was in fact a manager. I had not yet become someone they trusted. I was in management.

It took me a while to understand why that moment stuck with me. It wasn't just about people avoiding me at the end of the day, it was about something much deeper. I hadn't established who I was as a leader. I didn't set expectations for them, and I hadn't allowed them to set expectations for me either. I assumed that working hard and showing up would be enough. If I just kept doing what I'd always done, everything would fall into place. But leadership doesn't work that way. It requires clarity. It requires trust. And it requires you to show people what kind of leader you are and what matters to you, what they can count on you for, and how you want to work together. Without that, people make their own assumptions. And that's exactly what happened. I hadn't told them what I expected, and I hadn't asked them what they needed. We were just coexisting in silence. Me in my new role, them unsure of how to engage with it.

What I had to work through was that this silence created distance. Not because they didn't like me, they liked me the day before I was a manager. Also, it was not because they didn't want to work hard but because I hadn't created an environment where open communication and shared understanding could grow. I hadn't defined our team culture, because I hadn't defined who I was trying to be as a leader. That realization hit me harder than any feedback I've ever received. Because it wasn't about a specific task or a single moment, it was about everything I wasn't doing. Leadership isn't just about stepping into a new title. It's about stepping into a new responsibility: to set the tone, to create clarity, and to be consistent in who you are. Once I realized that, everything started to shift. I began to talk with the team, not just about work, but about how we work together. I asked questions, I shared my own expectations, and I invited feedback. And slowly, they stopped taking the long way around.

This scenario for me also made me realize that prior to being their manager I had set an expectation of who I would be as a manager by my actions prior to that. Had I been someone they felt they could trust leaving early maybe they would have carried that over into me being their manager now. Everything you do in some way, or another is being captured by others. A smile vs a frown, helping vs distancing, showing compassion vs being closed off. All your actions seen by others are bits of information that either consciously or subconsciously frame who you are as a colleague and will always carry over to who you are as a leader.

I was so focused on what I needed to say, what needed to get done, and how to move the team forward, that I wasn't always paying attention to what was happening around me. I'd miss the tension in the room, the person who had something to say but didn't feel comfortable speaking up, or the shift in energy that signaled we needed to slow down. Over time, I started to realize that leadership isn't just about driving to results, it's about reading the room, reading the people, and reading the moment. The environment is always giving you information, and great leaders learn how to pick up on it. They notice the tone, the body language, the silence, and the words that go unsaid. And the more I tuned in, the more effective I became, not because I changed what I believed, but because I adjusted how and when I delivered it. Situational awareness is what helps you lead with intention, not assumption.

Adjusting Your Approach Based on the Audience

Not everyone needs to hear the message the same way. Early on, I delivered everything the same, same tone, same level of detail, same sense of urgency. What I didn't realize was that my approach was only working for some people. Others needed more context. Some needed space to process. A few just needed the direct version and nothing else. I was treating everyone the way I would want to be led, instead of learning how they needed to be led. I decided one day to lead based on the person and the team, not based on me. It took me a while to get there.

I remember a moment when I delivered feedback to two team members in the exact same way. One of them appreciated the clarity. The other shut down completely. That was my wake-up call. It was a wake-up call for me because in my mind I realized I was literally treating each person the same and for a moment had forgotten who I was talking to and what my message was. There's an embarrassing story here where I had gotten further than I'd like to admit in a yearly review of one of my team before I realized I had been talking to the wrong person. Mistake made, significantly large mistake. I realized that part of leadership is being observant enough to recognize what kind of communication people respond to. It's not about being fake or changing who you are, it's about being flexible enough to be effective. That's what people need from their leader. Not someone who always says it the same way, but someone who knows how to say it, so it connects.

Now, I spend more time understanding the person than just delivering the message. I ask more questions. I pay attention to how they respond to different tones or formats. Do they like to think before they speak? Do they prefer bullet points or conversation? Once you figure that out, everything starts to click. Communication isn't one size that fits all. And the faster you figure out how to meet people where they are, the faster they'll follow you where you're trying to go.

Today I ensure to deliver a single message multiple times to multiple people in various formats. If one person doesn't fully consume the message, I'll reinforce it to them in their communication style in a one on one. If the message is worth communicating, it's worth ensuring it's communicated effectively no matter how much work that takes.

Reading the Room Before You Speak

I used to walk into meetings with a plan and a message, ready to go. I'd start speaking right away, thinking that being prepared meant jumping in and getting the ball rolling. But there were times when halfway through the meeting, I could feel something was off. People were disengaged. The tone didn't match the message. And I realized I wasn't reading the room. I was just reading my notes.

Reading the room means taking a moment to pause before you speak. Look around. Pay attention to who's leaning in and who's withdrawn. Who looks distracted, and who looks like they want to say something but won't. You can learn a lot in those few seconds before you say your first word. And sometimes what the room needs isn't what you planned. Maybe they need reassurance. Maybe they need more space to speak. Maybe they don't need another message at all, they need a moment to breathe.

Now I try to read the room before I try to lead the room. That little shift makes all the difference. Leadership isn't about pushing your message through it's about aligning your message with the moment. And you can't do that if you're not paying attention. Reading the room is a quiet skill, but it's one of the loudest signs of an intentional leader.

In a more remote workforce this gets more difficult. It means knowing your audience prior to the meeting. It means perhaps saying hello to each person to regain attentiveness or mood. If you're on camera this is much easier, if not you will need to work harder at this. I also now tend to start with the very simple yet effective practice of stating why we're in the meeting. "First let me ensure we're all on the same page" followed by an explanation of why we're there and what we hope to accomplish. That goes a long way in being an effective leader.

How to Tell When Your Message is Not Landing

One of the hardest parts of communication is realizing when it's not working. Sometimes your message doesn't land, and the room tells you, if you know what to look for. Blank stares, side glances, silence where there should be questions, or even forced nods. These are all signs that something's missing. But when you're too focused on delivering the message, you can miss the moment where you need to stop and pivot. My least liked phrase in a meeting is "can you repeat that I think I might have missed the question". Not because it's a genuine statement, but it normally comes after a simple question about what we've all been discussing for the last hour. This phrase in most situations means you lost that person and maybe more, a very long time ago.

I've learned to pause and ask myself, "Is this landing the way I think it is?" And if I'm not sure, I check in. I'll ask a clarifying question or open the floor with, "What's resonating here?" or "What's missing?" Not everyone will speak up, but it gives permission for people to express confusion or concern without feeling like they're challenging you. That small check-in can save a big misunderstanding down the road. We talked about silence previously too. There's something very loud about silence when you don't fill the gap to save anyone. When you ask, "What's missing?", wait as long as is needed to let the silence wake people up who may have drifted. Also don't be afraid to call on people individually. You'll find out who may have drifted and who hasn't.

There's a humility that comes with realizing your message didn't hit the mark. But it's not a failure, it's a signal. A chance to slow down, recalibrate, and try again. The goal isn't to say it once and move on. The goal is to be heard and understood. And sometimes that means adjusting mid-conversation. The best leaders don't just talk, they listen while they're talking.

Notice What is Being Said

Paying close attention to what people are saying seems obvious, but we often miss it. We listen to respond, not to understand. We hear the words, but not the meaning. I've been in meetings where someone voiced concern or gave feedback, and I nodded along without really taking it in. Later, when the issue came back up, I realized I didn't listen the first time. I heard them, but I didn't listen.

Now, when someone speaks, I try to stay present. Not just for the sake of being polite, but because what they're saying usually points to something deeper. A concern about a process might be a sign of burnout. A question about priorities might be a request for clarity. People rarely say exactly what they mean on the surface, you must listen for what's underneath.

Leadership means listening like it matters, because it does. What people say gives your insight into how they think, how they feel, and what they need. But you must be willing to slow down long enough to hear it. It's not about catching every word; it's about catching the meaning behind the message.

Notice What's Not Being Said

What's not being said is often louder than what is being said. I didn't understand this until I started paying attention to the silence in the room. The people who didn't speak up. The topics that kept getting brushed aside. The conversations that ended a little too quickly. At first, I thought everything was fine if no one said anything, there must be no problem, right? Wrong. Sometimes silence is safety. Sometimes silence is fear. And as a leader, if you're not looking for it, you'll miss it.

Noticing what's not being said means looking at who's quiet when they're usually vocal. It means recognizing when a tough subject gets avoided again and again. It means asking follow-up questions, not just accepting the surface answer. I've learned that just because someone doesn't speak up doesn't mean they don't have something to say, it might just mean they don't think it's safe to say it.

Creating space for what's unsaid is part of building trust. You can't force people to speak, but you can create an environment where they want to. Where they know they'll be heard, not judged. That's where the real conversations start. That's where leadership shows up, in the listening that happens beyond words. Because what's not said might just be the most important thing you need to hear.

Lessons Learned

I used to think leadership was about having the answers and making things happen. But I've learned that some of the most important parts of leadership come from simply paying attention. Situational awareness really noticing what's happening around you changed how I lead. Early on, I missed the signs. I missed the silence, the hesitation, the discomfort. I thought working hard and showing up was enough, but I hadn't taken the time to read the room or understand how others were responding to me in my new role. That was a hard realization, but it was also the turning point.

Leadership isn't just about delivering messages it's about knowing when and how to deliver them. It's not just about hearing what's said, it's about listening to what's not. Whether it's reading the energy in a meeting, adjusting your message based on the person, or picking up on unspoken tension, being situationally aware helps you lead with intention. It builds trust, creates connection, and ensures that you're not just pushing forward, but bringing people with you. Once I stopped leading from habit and started leading with awareness, I saw everything more clearly and so did the people around me.

Introduction To Conscientiousness

Conscientiousness, to me, is doing the right thing even when no one is watching. It goes beyond reliability or organization, it's about follow-through, attention to detail, and taking pride in the quality of your work. Early in my career, I equated effectiveness with hitting deadlines and staying busy. Over time, I learned that true impact lies in how you show up, especially when it's inconvenient. It's answering the difficult email, double-checking your work without being asked, and finishing tasks the right way, not just the fastest way. Conscientiousness is rooted in consistency, integrity, and a respect for your work, your team, and yourself. It may not always be visible, but it builds trust over time and trust is the foundation of leadership.

When Abraham Lincoln became president, he famously made the deliberate choice to appoint his strongest political rivals to his Cabinet, men who had criticized him publicly and competed against him. He knew leading a divided nation required more than loyalty; it demanded competence, diversity of thought, and a commitment to the greater good. That decision wasn't easy or popular, but it was rooted in integrity and responsibility. Lincoln prioritized the mission over ego, showing that true leadership means making thoughtful, sometimes difficult choices that serve others, not just yourself.

I gained a deeper understanding of this when I left Ericsson to join Perot Systems Corporation, an IT services provider. At the time, I made the unexpected decision to move from a management role back to an individual contributor position, both within email support. I was surrounded by highly technical, specifically focused, yet meaningful and collaborative focused people. At Perot Systems, I was supporting multiple clients, each with their own systems, requirements, and expectations. It was a highly structured and efficient environment that demanded adaptability and precision. I had to learn to manage shifting priorities, deliver across various client needs, and operate without shortcuts. It was here that I truly learned the value of being conscientious, how to manage my time, communicate clearly, and execute consistently at a high standard.

My time at Perot Systems was short, just two years, but significant. I eventually moved into a management role; I had a team again. It was during this period that I began to consider leadership as more than a title; it might be my path. That experience prepared me for my next opportunity at Cadbury Schweppes. Returning to a large, global organization came with new complexity: a broader scale, a faster pace, and a more collaborative enterprise environment. Thankfully, my time at Ericsson provided a reference point, and my growth at Perot gave me the tools to step in with confidence. In hindsight, I wished I had paid more attention at Ericsson, I now understood how valuable that early exposure to a global operation truly was.

Interestingly, I once again chose to leave a managerial role to become an individual contributor at Cadbury. At the time, I struggled with the balance between being technical and taking on leadership responsibilities. I didn't fully understand what leadership meant. I was managing work, not leading people. It wasn't until much later in my time at Cadbury that I began to grasp the difference. Leadership isn't just about output, it's about vision, influence, and creating an environment where others can succeed.

Each of these roles taught me that conscientiousness isn't just about what you do, it's about how you do it. When you show up with care, consistency, and a deep sense of ownership, people notice. And while every new organization meant starting fresh and rebuilding trust, I came to understand that the way I carried myself, the way I honored the details and followed through, was what helped people believe in me.

The upcoming section on Conscientiousness outlines the mindset and habits I've learned to focus on to become a better leader. These are the principles that have helped me build trust, deliver with integrity, and create impact, not just once, but consistently over time.

The Leadership Mindset

I thought leadership came after experience, after recognition, after someone gave you permission to lead. But the truth is, leadership starts the moment you decide to lead yourself differently. That means taking responsibility for your effort, your attitude, and how you show up especially when it is easier not to. That mindset shift didn't happen overnight for me. It happened in the quiet choices taking the initiative when I could've waited, asking questions when I felt unsure, helping others even when I was busy. Those weren't big leadership moments, but they were foundational ones. And over time, they shaped how others saw me and more importantly, how I saw myself.

Mindset is what carries you when nothing else is certain. It's what keeps you growing, even when no one is noticing. I've found that the people who become great leaders aren't always the smartest or most experienced, they're the ones who keep showing up, keep learning, and keep pushing themselves to be just a little better than yesterday. They lead from the inside out. And once you adopt that mindset, you stop waiting for leadership to be handed to you. You start building it from the ground up, making one decision at a time.

The idea of not just bringing problems, but bringing solutions is a big one when it comes to being a leader in any role. I used to think that pointing out an issue was enough that identifying something broken would show I was paying attention. But over time, I realized that true leadership isn't just about spotting the cracks. It's about stepping into them with ideas, energy, and a willingness to try. When you come to the table with potential solutions, you show that you care enough to think things through. You move from someone who points out what's wrong to someone others trust to help make it right. And even if your solution isn't the final answer, your effort still shifts the tone. It turns the conversation from frustration to progress. That's the kind of mindset that builds momentum.

During my time at Cadbury and early into my transition at Kraft, I approached problem-solving the wrong way. I had the right intentions but the wrong execution. Instead of seeking answers, I would dig through discussions trying to find where something had gone wrong, often focusing more on assigning blame than uncovering the real issue. I was quick to question the technology or the person behind it, rather than pausing to understand the root cause or ask how we could fix it together. I had to learn to shift my mindset from antagonist to protagonist, from someone trying to catch a mistake to someone committed to solving it. Once I made that shift, it changed everything. I began to collaborate differently. I connected more meaningfully with others, and problem-solving became less about proving a point and more about making progress. That mindset unlocked a level of teamwork and trust I hadn't experienced before, and it made me a far more effective and respected leader.

Another shift happened when I started thinking of the company I worked for as if it were my own. I learned this when working in a grocery store during high school. As a sacker, I also had other responsibilities. When it wasn't busy, my job was anything my manager told me to do, cleaning spills, stocking shelves, organizing carts, you name it. One day, I was tossing a case of canned goods onto the shelf a little too carelessly and dented more than a few. I didn't think much of it at the time. To me, it was just part of the job, some products got damaged, that's normal, right? But later, my manager pulled me aside and walked me over to the damaged goods cart. It was overflowing.

He looked at me and said, "If this was your store, would you be OK with this?" And it stuck with me. He wasn't angry, he was teaching me something I didn't know I needed to learn. That damaged product meant lost profit. Lost profit meant tighter budgets. And that trickled down to all of us, hours, raises, store upgrades. I had never connected the dots before. I was just doing my job. But after that moment, I started paying attention differently. I handled items with more care, I also took pride in the appearance of the store. Not because someone was watching, but because I realized it mattered. Treating the store like it was mine didn't mean acting like I owned it, it meant caring enough to act like it mattered. That mindset stuck with me long after I left that job. It's one of those early lessons that ended up meaning more than I ever expected.

Defining Your Why, Purpose as A Compass

There was a stretch early in my career where I was just grinding. Doing the work, chasing the goals, and hoping the next role would give me some sense of meaning. I chased praise and rewards. But even when I hit milestones, something still felt off. That's when I realized I didn't have a clear "why." I was operating on autopilot. Getting clarity on my purpose didn't mean I had all the answers, but it gave me direction. It reminded me that leadership isn't just about getting things done, it's about what you're doing it for. That clarity changed how I approached the people around me, too. Purpose brings consistency. It helps you lead with integrity, because you're not chasing outcomes, you're leading from values.

When I finally sat down to write out what mattered to me most, what I stood for as a leader I found that it wasn't a job title or a promotion. It was impact. It was helping others grow. It was building trust and showing up in a way that made things better for the people I worked with. That became my filter for decisions. If something didn't align with that, I passed. If it did, I leaned all the way in. And once I started leading with that kind of clarity, the right opportunities started to find me not because I was trying to impress anyone, but because I finally knew what I stood for.

I want to take on new challenges and for me that means taller mountains to climb. It also means turning the reigns over to someone else when they're ready to move up. I used to fear replacement. Now I fear stagnation. There's a section in chapter three that goes into more detail on this but for now just know that you should be trying to make yourself replaceable. That's my new purpose and that purpose has given me more clarity than I've ever had.

The Power of Influence, Someone's Always Influencing Someone

One thing I've come to realize is that influence happens long before you ever speak a word. It's how you respond to pressure, how you treat people when no one's watching, and how you carry yourself day after day. I've worked with leaders who didn't say much, but their presence said everything. You knew where they stood by the way they showed up. On the flip side, I've also worked with people in leadership roles who had the title, but not the influence because people didn't trust them. Influence isn't given it's earned, and it's earned in moments you don't even realize are being watched. That's the part no one tells you. You're always leading someone. And the standard you hold for yourself sets the tone for the people around you.

I started paying attention to how I influenced others not just when I had a platform, but when I didn't. Was I consistent? Did I encourage people? Did I follow through on what I said? Influence, to me, is about integrity. It's about being someone people trust enough to follow. Not because they must, but because they want to. And once you understand the weight of that, you take more care with your words, your tone, and your presence. You start leading in the way people need not just in the way that feels natural to you.

What's equally important to realize is that you're not the only one doing the influencing, others are shaping you too, whether you notice it or not. Influence is something we absorb just by being around it. I've picked up countless leadership habits from people I never formally reported to. The way they handled tough conversations, the patience they showed in meetings, the way they treated people when there was no obvious benefit to doing so, those moments stuck with me. And that's what makes influence so powerful. You don't need a title to model behavior that others take with them. You don't always know when it's happening, but the people around you are learning from you. And you're learning from them, one quiet moment at a time.

One example that sticks with me happened when I was talking to a leader about network security. I used a simple analogy: you can have multiple locks on the doors in your house, but if all the locks use the same key, you're not as secure as you think. Sometime later, I was in another meeting, and that same leader used the analogy to explain the importance of layered security but instead of referencing doors, he said windows. The metaphor was a bit off, but I didn't correct him because it worked for him and this situation. At that moment, I realized something more important, my message had landed. I had influenced how he thought, how he explained, and how he would now influence others. That's when I really understood the value of influence you can't always see. It doesn't always show up as credit or recognition, it shows up in the ideas that stick, the behaviors that spread, and the culture that slowly starts to shift around you.

I also remember a time I was influenced without even realizing it in the moment. Back to my JCPenney days, I worked with a leader who had this quiet but incredibly effective habit of taking detailed notes during every one-on-one meeting. At first, I just noticed how prepared she always seemed how she could refer to something I mentioned weeks ago, follow up on a detail I'd forgotten, or tee up a conversation for the next meeting based on a thread we hadn't finished. What I didn't realize at the time was that her approach was shaping mine. Slowly, I started doing the same, bringing notes, following up more intentionally, and preparing for the next discussion instead of just reacting in the moment. I never told her she influenced me. I'm not even sure she knew. But that simple act of showing up prepared, week after week, made me better. And it reminded me that influence isn't always about what you say, it's often about the consistency of what you do.

Showing Up with Intention Leading on Purpose, Not by Habit

Leading with intention doesn't mean over thinking everything. It means slowing down long enough to make sure your actions line up with your purpose. I used to rely on habits to get through the same meetings, same talking points, same approach. But I realized that habit could lead to autopilot. And when you're on autopilot, you miss moments that matter. I had to ask myself: Am I showing up with purpose, or just a presence? That question changed how I started meetings, how I gave feedback, and how I supported my team. I stopped doing things just because they'd always been done that way and started asking if they were helping.

When you lead with intention, people notice. You're not just going through the motions you're making space for what matters. You take time to prepare. You ask better questions. You respond instead of reacting. And maybe most importantly, you set the tone for your team to do the same. Intention is contagious. It shows others that you value the moment, and that you value them. And over time, those intentional moments build into something much bigger a culture where people feel seen, respected, and motivated to lead alongside you.

There was a moment in my career when I finally became comfortable with the sound of my own voice. It wasn't until later in my career, not until the last five years. Up until that point, I was always second-guessing what I wanted to say wondering if it was the right moment, the right phrasing, or if I'd come across the wrong way. I was afraid of saying something that sounded stupid, so I often said nothing at all. But during a team strategy session, I had an idea that felt important, and for the first time, I didn't talk myself out of sharing it. I spoke up. I said it clearly and confidently. And while it wasn't perfect, it was mine and it added value to the discussion. That moment wasn't just about sharing an idea, it was about learning to trust myself as a leader. From that point on, I stopped waiting for permission to lead and started leaning into my voice with more intent.

What changed after that was subtle but powerful. I led meetings with more purpose. I gave feedback even when it was hard. I asked questions not just to gather information, but to push the conversation forward. I also became more open to acknowledging when I got something wrong. Leading with intention doesn't mean getting it right every time, it means being willing to own your missteps, learn from them, and keep going. And when your team sees you doing that, it gives them permission to do the same. That's the kind of environment I want to create, one where people feel safe enough to speak up, bold enough to take the initiative, and confident enough to lead, even in the small moments. Because when you show up with intention, you invite others to do the same. And that's where real leadership lives.

Lessons Learned

What I've learned is that leadership doesn't start with a title, it starts with mindset. It's the decision to show up differently, to take ownership of your growth, and to lead from wherever you are. Early on, I thought being a leader meant waiting for permission or recognition. But over time, I realized the real work of leadership begins the moment you stop asking for those things and start acting with intention. It's in the small choices and how you treat others, how you respond under pressure, and whether you show up with purpose or out of habit that your leadership takes shape.

Understanding my purpose helped me shift from just working hard to working with direction. Once I got clear on what mattered to me, helping others grow, building trust, showing up with integrity, everything changed. Influence, too, showed up in ways I didn't expect. I've learned that you're always influencing and being influenced, even when you don't realize it. That's why consistency, preparation, and presence matter. Whether it was adopting someone else's good habits or seeing my own ideas reflected in others, I began to see leadership not as something I stepped into but as something I lived into. And the more I leaned into that intention, the more I grew. That's the foundation I keep coming back to, lead yourself first, and everything else starts to follow.

Working Hard Pays Off

It's Not Just the Grind, it's The Intent

There's a belief early in your career that working hard means grinding non-stop. Long hours, skipping breaks, answering emails late at night. I used to think that too. That if I wasn't constantly busy, I wasn't showing value. But what I've learned is that working hard isn't about exhaustion, it's about presence. It's about doing the job you've been asked to do to the best of your ability, every day, without needing constant praise to keep going. And when you start thinking about work that way, everything shifts. I used to hear stories about leaders in my company that worked all day and night. I once heard a story that our CIO slept with his laptop next to his bed and if an email came in while he was sleeping, he'd hear it and respond. At the time I believed it but it could not possibly have been true. These are the stories we all hear that make us tense when thinking this is what it takes to succeed. I'm here to tell you it's not. It's hard work, yes, but it's not difficult work.

Being a hard worker doesn't mean being the loudest or the last to leave. It means being dependable. It means showing up prepared, staying focused, and following through. It means asking thoughtful questions and doing the work without cutting corners. You don't have to run on empty to prove your worth. You must be consistent and intentional in how you show up. When you approach each task like it matters, no matter how small, people notice. That's what separates good from great. It's not about pace, it's about purpose.

If you want to move forward in your career, you must show value. That doesn't mean you say yes to everything, or that you're the busiest person in the room. It means you're smart with your time, clear in your priorities, and committed to quality. Working smart is part of it knowing where to focus and when to speak up. But working hard is what builds your reputation. Over time, people begin to trust that when you're involved, things will get done right. That's not something you announce, it's something you prove, over and over.

I've hired people based on work ethics alone. Not because they knew everything, but because I knew they'd figure it out. That kind of trust doesn't come from being flashy, it comes from showing up, being reliable, and doing the work like it matters. Because it does. You don't have to be perfect. You just must be present, willing, and ready to grow. That's what hard work really looks like. And that's how careers are built from the ground up, one intentional effort at a time.

Say Yes to Experiences, and Volunteer

Early in my IT career, I said yes to just about everything I could. Not because I had the time or even the confidence, I just knew that the more I put myself in the room, the more I'd learn. I volunteered to help build servers, run network cables, unbox equipment, anything that let me be near the work. I wasn't the expert. I wasn't always sure what was going on. But I knew one thing: being close to people who knew more than me would always push me to grow. And every time I said yes, I took something away I didn't know the day before. I learned this lesson in my early days at Ericsson and it was a theme I carried with me in each role. I'm thankful I had supporters who didn't mind allowing me to engage when I wasn't adding any real value. I strive to pay this forward to this day. If someone is willing to learn we should all be willing to teach.

There were times I joined issue resolution calls simply to observe and learn. I remained quiet, fully engaged, and focused on understanding how teams navigated high-pressure situations. Watching how leaders communicated, managed stress, and worked through complex problems offered insights that no manual or training could replicate. I wasn't there to be seen; I was there to grow. Over time, my presence alone began to speak for itself. I became known as someone who consistently showed up, demonstrated curiosity, and cared enough to invest in learning, even when I didn't have all the answers. The truth is, you gain far more from observing rare, high-impact scenarios than from routine ones. Great leaders build a wide-ranging perspective and that starts by taking every opportunity to be present. Those moments are where real development happens.

Saying yes to experience doesn't always mean leading the effort. Sometimes it means being the quiet one who's paying attention. The person willing to lend a hand without needing a spotlight. Those yeses added up. People started inviting me to more conversations, asking for my help with projects, pulling me in because they knew I wanted to grow. That's how you build momentum in your career not by waiting until you feel ready, but by saying yes before you are, and trusting the experience will meet you halfway.

The more experiences you say yes to, the more doors you open. And the more you learn not just about the job, but about yourself. You learn where you thrive, what motivates you, what challenges you. Most of all, you show others that you're someone who doesn't sit back, you step in. That's what leadership looks like in its early stages. Not in the title, but in the willingness to say, "I'll help," even when you don't have all the answers. Especially then.

The Commitment to Level Up

Mid-way through my career; I was looking forward to a promotion that felt like the obvious next step. I had been doing good work, showing up, and thought I was ready. So, when I had the conversation with my manager and expressed my interest, I expected a clear road map or at least some encouragement. What I got instead was a phrase I didn't fully understand at the time: "Do the job to get the job." At first, it felt like a brush-off. If I'm not in the role, how can I do the job? But over time, I realized that wasn't just advice, it was a challenge. A challenge to step up, to commit to something bigger than my title, and to show I could deliver at the next level before someone handed it to me. That's when I started to understand what commitment really looks like. I'll admit though, at first, I just got upset. It took me longer than I care to admit realizing that statements meaning and value. When it finally sank in, I treated all my roles in this way. From then on, not only did I do my role, but I mentally put myself in the role of my manager. There's a section later where I go into more detail on the importance of not always asking your manager for guidance, and thinking on your own.

There's a gap between where you are today and the next level of your career. Everyone has that gap; it doesn't matter if you're just starting out or if you've been in the same role for years. The difference between those who close that gap and those who don't is commitment. Not just working longer hours or doing what's expected but showing a consistent willingness to step beyond what's comfortable. That's where the next level lives.

I've seen it in others, and I've experienced it myself. You reach the point that doing your job well is no longer enough, you must start doing the things that prepare you for the job you want. That might mean learning a new skill on your own time, volunteering for a project outside your role, or asking for feedback you're not totally ready to hear. It might mean leading a meeting for the first time, even if it scares you, or mentoring someone else, even if you're still figuring things out yourself. These moments don't just test your commitment, they shape your readiness.

Moving up doesn't happen by accident. It happens because you commit to doing the work that no one sees right away. Because you believe in your own growth enough to put in the reps before the results show up. Hard work is the foundation, but commitment is what turns that effort into real progress. You don't need to have it all figured out, you just need to be all in. And if you can do that consistently, the next level doesn't feel like a leap. It feels like the natural next step.

Creating the Circle of Leadership Takes Effort

There's a point in your career where the shift happens. At first, you're the one asking all the questions, listening to meetings, quietly observing how others lead. But if you stick with it if you say yes to the right experiences, if you work hard and show up with purpose eventually someone turns to you with a question of their own. That's the moment you realize you've become the one people look at. You're no longer just learning from others, you're teaching too. And that's where the leadership circle begins.

Creating that circle of leadership means understanding that knowledge isn't something you hoard, it's something you pass on. I've had people bring me into their world, let me listen, let me mess up, and let me ask the same question more than once. I owe a lot to those moments. That's why now, when someone newer to the team asks if they can shadow or need help with something I've done a hundred times, I stop what I'm doing. Because I remember what it felt like to be on the other side of that learning curve, and I know how much one moment of patience can mean.

Teaching others also sharpens your own skills. You start to understand your decisions better when you must explain them. You see gaps in your process you didn't notice before. You realize that leading someone else through a challenge gives you clarity on how you lead yourself. There's growth on both sides. That's what makes it a circle not just a hand off, but a continual flow of learning, sharing, and evolving together.

When you're intentional about creating this circle, you build more than just individual skills you build culture. One where people help each other, where growth is shared, and where leadership isn't tied to a title. It's about behavior. Influence. And legacy. And the best part is, the more you teach, the more you learn. That's leadership at its best, lifting others while continuing to rise.

One of the most important moments in my growth came from an unexpected place. I had stalled in my career and constantly butted heads with a peer, someone who challenged me at every opportunity. We didn't see eye to eye, and I often saw our disagreements as roadblocks. There was one moment when we both got called into our manager's office because we had got into a voice raising incident in front of others. It was that bad. Our manager basically said stop acting like children and figure it out on your own, or he'd figure it out for us. You never want your boss to make that statement. We went our separate ways, didn't play nice together but tolerated each other. It was awkward and stayed that way until I swallowed my pride, saw a true opportunity and asked him to mentor me. That shift changed everything. I didn't just hear his perspective, I truly listened. I began to understand his methodology, his reasoning, and the way he approached problems differently than I did. What happened next was bigger than just improved collaboration. We became better colleagues, built mutual respect, and I grew into a more well-rounded leader because of it. Sometimes leadership development doesn't come from being the strongest voice in the room, it comes from listening to the one you've been resisting the most. That's how the circle expands when you allow yourself to be taught by those who once challenged you.

Rinse and Repeat

There's a moment in every career when you finally figure out something that works. A way you prep for meetings. A style of communication that lands well. A system to keep yourself organized. Whatever it is, it clicks. You feel in control. You feel confident. That's not luck that's progress. And when you find those things that help you succeed, the smartest move you can make is to do them again. And again. That's the rinse and repeat of leadership.

We often think growth means constantly reinventing ourselves. And yes, learning and adapting are essential but so is consistency. Once you've found a rhythm that works, lean into it. Build on it. If you have a prep routine that keeps you grounded before big meetings, don't treat it like a one-time win, make it your standard. If taking five minutes after a one-on-one to write down key takeaways helps you follow through, then protect that habit like it's part of your job. Because it is.

The rinse and repeat mindset isn't about being rigid, it's about being reliable. It shows others that you're not just effective once, you're effective consistently. That kind of dependability is what builds trust. It's what turns good leaders into great ones. Over time, your repeatable processes become part of your leadership signature. They're the small things that make a big impact. And when people know they can count on you to show up with clarity, preparation, and follow-through every time, that's when your influence starts to multiply. You don't have to be flashy, just faithful to what works. That's where real conscientious leadership lives.

The key is staying long enough in something to know whether it's a one-off reaction or a trend. You'll never find what works if you constantly change based on every bit of friction. But you also can't be so locked in that you ignore feedback altogether. The balance is learning to recognize when something just needs time and when it needs a tune-up. Stick with your approach long enough to learn from it, not just react to it. That's how you build confident, effective leadership habits that stand the test of time.

Lessons Learned

Hard work isn't about burning yourself out or staying the latest just to be seen, it's about being intentional, reliable, and present in everything you do. What matters most isn't how many hours you put in, but the quality of those hours and the value you bring with them. Being consistent, showing up prepared, and taking pride in the work you've been asked to do earns trust over time and separates those who are ready for more from those who are just going through the motions.

Saying yes to opportunities, especially when you're unsure or just starting out, is how you grow. The more you expose yourself to real-world learning even if you're silent in the room the more experience you gain and the more visible your commitment becomes. You're not just building knowledge, you're building momentum. That willingness to learn, support, and step in lays the foundation for leadership before any title ever does.

Progress in your career takes commitment. It takes possessing the idea that to move up, you first must show you're already operating at the next level. That doesn't mean faking it, it means growing into it. And along the way, the relationships you build and the experiences you say yes form the circle of leadership where you learn from others and give back just the same. What you repeat becomes your reputation. What you commit to becomes your character. And what you choose to learn from, even the hard stuff, becomes your leadership story.

Helping others

First Lead Yourself

There was a stretch early in my career where, across multiple companies, looking back, I honestly don't remember being managed much at all. I know I had a manager, I reported to someone, but I can't recall any moment where they were checking in constantly, telling me what to do, or guiding me step by step. That space wasn't neglected, looking back on it I must assume it was trust. I was responsible for resolving support tickets, and I knew what my job was. So, I did it. Every day. I learned quickly that no one was going to walk me through it. If something was broken, I had to fix it. If I didn't know the answer, I had to figure it out or find someone who did. That level of autonomy forced me to become accountable not just to a manager, but to myself. It wasn't about being told what to do it was about becoming someone who didn't need to be told.

One of the most defining experiences during that time was when I was asked to support a customer on-site every week, for months. At Perot Systems we were an extension of their company in that we provided them 24/7 support. Their team was short-handed, and we filled in until they could hire someone long term. I traveled there consistently, acted as the primary point of contact, and handled whatever they needed. There was no script. No play book. Just the expectation that I'd show up and figure it out. And that's exactly what I did. I reported back weekly if anything major happened and that's about it. That experience shaped how I approached work. At the time I was not focused on my career I was only focused on each day and getting through it. I learned how to lead myself by sometimes recognizing I was just going through the motions without anyone around. However, that started to change when the customer asked me questions about daily issues or brought me escalations. Suddenly without being in charge I was. I had to learn how to assess a situation, make decisions, and build trust with the customer without waiting for instruction. I didn't realize it at the time, but that was the beginning of me developing a leadership mindset not because I was managing others, but because I had learned how to manage myself. Regardless of what role you're currently in these opportunities exist and need to be acknowledged.

When it came time to hire the long-term person for that customer site, I ended up interviewing and selecting the candidate myself. It felt like passing the torch, but with care. I knew I wouldn't be there forever, so my focus shifted to setting them up for success not by giving them all the answers, but by giving them room to find their own. I made a point to guide them, share what I'd learned, and be available for support, but I also stepped back enough to let them lead in their own way. They were going to be the one building those relationships long term, and they needed to feel empowered to make decisions. That balance of support and space is something I still carry with me in leadership today.

There's something profoundly impactful about preparing your own replacement. It's a mark of mature leadership rooted in humility, intentionality, and long-term thinking. It takes clarity to invest in someone else's growth and confidence to know that developing others doesn't diminish your value, it multiplies it. When done well, it's one of the most rewarding outcomes of leadership, leaving something better than you found it, and knowing it will continue to thrive without you. This is a statement I can make now; I didn't see the true value of it at the time.

Help Without Hovering

It was around this time when I learned that helping doesn't always mean doing. I thought being a good leader meant stepping in whenever someone on my team was struggling, giving advice, offering solutions, even taking over tasks when needed. After all, that's what a leader does right? Not really. What I didn't realize then was that sometimes, too much help becomes interference. What starts as support can quietly turn into micromanagement, and that's not leadership, that's control.

I had to learn how to pause before jumping in. I started asking myself, does this person need help, or do they just need space to figure it out? That shift changed everything. I began focusing on being present without being overbearing, offering help, but not hovering. Being available, but not always inserting myself. The real test was learning how to trust my team to take ownership, even if that meant they might stumble a little along the way.

One moment stands out. A team member was giving a presentation on the status of our department for the month, their first. I could've taken the lead. I knew the material, knew what they wanted to hear and how. But instead, I let them own it. I gave them the support, the prep, the safety net if needed but I didn't interfere. They crushed it. And what came from that moment shaped us both, they walked away with a new level of confidence and experience, knowing they could lead and be heard, and I walked away realizing that real leadership is about stepping back so others can step forward. Another turning point not just in their growth, but in their mind toward becoming the kind of leader who builds leaders, not just completes tasks.

That's what leadership is about. Not doing it for them. Not disappearing either. It's walking beside someone, not in front of them. Helping without hovering means knowing your presence matters but so does your restraint.

Support vs. Control, How to Help Without Taking Over

Support and control can look dangerously similar in leadership if you're not careful. You step in to help, offer guidance, maybe even take on a task or two to keep things moving but before you know it, you're the one driving the outcome, not your team. I've learned that offering help doesn't mean taking over. It means creating space for someone else to grow, while being close enough to catch them if they stumble. True support is rooted in trust. It's saying, "I believe you can do this," and then stepping back to let them prove it, even if they don't get it perfect the first time. I still struggle with this, I will fall into the mode of just doing it because it needs done. When I chose to step in and do the task one of my team didn't it's for good reason. For example, if that person is overwhelmed or it's a time bound requirement. If that happens, I always try to at least allow them to review and provide feedback. As much as possible while stepping in to help I ensure they know that they could have done it or will learn from me doing it. I too do not think I'm the best at anything so as much as possible getting feedback helps me as well.

The problem is, when you blur that line and move from supporting to controlling, you take away ownership. And with it, confidence. I've been guilty of this. I've jumped in too early, rewritten the email, fixed the slide deck, made the call because it was faster or easier. But all I really did was communicate to my team that I didn't trust them to figure it out. That moment may solve a short-term issue, but it creates long term doubt. People stop stepping up. They wait for you to take the lead. And then you wonder why no one owns the work. The answer is that you never let them. The next time the same task comes up and they don't do it could be because they assume you'll do it again. Ensure to set the tone and expectation of this task vs any future one. For example, letting them know you stepped in this time but going forward "you own this" is a clear message on future completion of that same task.

Real leadership means offering your presence, your insight, and your encouragement, without taking the wheel. It's letting someone else run with an idea, knowing they'll ask for help if they need it. It's sitting in the discomfort of watching someone navigate a challenge you could easily solve, because you know the lesson will stick more if they find their way through it. Support isn't silent, but it's also not control. It's the balance of being available, without being overbearing. And when you get that balance right, you not only grow your team's capability, you grow their confidence.

Respecting Roles, Boundaries as a Form of Leadership Discipline

Respecting the boundaries of your team's roles is one of the most disciplined forms of leadership. It's easy to step in, especially when you've done the job before or feel the pressure of getting it right. But leadership isn't about doing it, it's about enabling. When you respect someone's role, you're not just staying in your lane, you're giving them ownership, autonomy, and the room to grow. That distance isn't detachment. It's intentional space that tells your team, I trust you to lead your part.

One of the ways I've found to strike this balance is by making it clear that while I'm not hovering, I'm always available. I let my team know that at any moment they can reach out for a quick sync whether it's to validate an approach, talk through a challenge, or just check alignment. And because that can't be left to chance, I've built recurring one-on-one meetings into the structure of our week. These aren't status updates. They're dedicated moments for check-ins, coaching, or simply asking, how are you doing with all of this? That regular cadence allows for support without intrusion. It keeps the connection strong, without stepping into the territory they've been trusted to lead.

Leadership boundaries aren't about stepping back they're about knowing when to step in. And the clearer you are about those boundaries, the more empowered your team becomes. It's discipline, not distance, that builds trust. Working as a team means understanding that individual success is only part of the equation. Every win, every challenge overcome, contributes to something greater than any one person, it contributes to the team's success.

As a leader, giving your team autonomy isn't about creating silos, it's about helping them think bigger. When people begin to see their role not just as their work, but as our progress, they begin leading with a broader perspective. They start making decisions that support the group, not just themselves. That's how leaders are built, by learning that growth isn't about standing out, it's about lifting the whole team.

When Not Helping Is Helping, Resisting the Hero Instinct

I think we all know the person who likes to save the day. The mentality that you can't be a hero without a good issue. And they seem to hover around issues and then swoop in to save the day. What I've recognized is that it's a trait not many leaders have. Good leaders let individuals learn and grow with course corrections along the way. A good leader does not allow an issue, they strive to prevent them. The more responsibility you take on the more this becomes not only imperative but should be your mantra. It's not that you don't help, it's that you know when to.

There's an instinct that kicks in when you see someone on your team struggling, the urge to jump in, fix it, and save the day. I used to lean into that instinct hard. I thought that being a good leader meant being the hero. But over time, I learned that constantly stepping in doesn't just fix the problem, it robs someone of the opportunity to learn how to fix it themselves. That's not leadership, that's dependence. And if you're not careful, you end up being the bottleneck, not the support.

One of the hardest things to learn as a leader is when not helping is the best kind of help. Letting someone wrestle with a problem, stumble through the process, or even make a mistake can feel counterintuitive. But those controlled stumbles are where real growth happens. You don't want your team to avoid mistakes at all costs. You want them to understand that mistakes are part of the process as long as they're learning, adjusting, and not repeating the same ones. That's how confidence is built. That's how capability is developed.

The key is in creating a space where mistakes are safe to make but not safe to ignore. You're not abandoning your team you're guiding from a distance. You're letting them know that you're there, that you trust them, and that you believe in their ability to figure it out. And when they do, that sense of ownership and pride will carry farther than anything you could have done for them. The hero's instinct might feel good in the moment but resisting it might be the most empowering move you can make as a leader.

Lessons Learned

Helping others as a leader is not about doing the work for them, it's about creating the conditions where others can succeed, grow, and learn to lead themselves. One of the biggest lessons I've learned is that autonomy builds accountability. Early in my career, I wasn't micromanaged, and at the time I didn't realize the trust that had been placed in me. But it taught me something foundational: how to lead myself. That trust empowered me to figure things out, take ownership, and make decisions and it was those moments that quietly built the core of my leadership mindset.

As I progressed in my career, I came to understand that helping others requires balance. It means being supportive without being controlling, and present without being overbearing. Whether it was letting a team member take the lead on a big presentation, mentoring someone I once clashed with, or resisting the urge to fix a problem myself, I've learned that stepping back can sometimes be the greatest form of leadership. Letting others figure it out with guidance nearby, but not overshadowing builds capability, confidence, and long-term success for the individual and the team.

Leadership isn't about saving the day it's about building the people who will. That means creating space for mistakes, for problem-solving, and for growth. The real reward isn't in being the hero. It's in seeing someone else rise, knowing you had a hand in shaping that moment without needing to take the credit. That's the power of helping with purpose where trust, patience, and humility drive the impact far beyond what any task alone ever could.

Using Yes

When You Already Know the Answer is Yes

We've all experienced those moments when we know what we need to do but for some inherent emotional reason we fight the urge to say yes. Can you work late to help the team finish a project that's due first thing tomorrow? You may have worked more than anyone on the team to this point. Unless you have an urgent prior engagement you absolutely can't get out of, you know the right response is to say yes. Some however don't. I've seen too many people in this same situation say they can't and make up an excuse. Let's all be transparent here; most people can spot a made-up excuse no matter how crafty it was created.

For example, I knew a guy who used to set up his sick days in advance. He'd want to take off Friday but it's too late to ask off and there are things at work that need his attention. On Thursday he'd start the rouse. Let a couple of people know he's just not feeling great. Tomorrow when I, I mean he, calls out sick no one's the wiser and they're all just hoping that he makes a speedy recovery and how sad that he was sick over the weekend. The truth is that this never works in the long run. Most if not all immediately see through it as well. Say yes, don't say no, and don't make things up. People see through this, I promise you.

Opportunities at work come by all the time if you're looking for them. If you're a person who says yes consistently then they're always around. If you look for a way to say no, you're missing out. From a career perspective, if you can say yes, it's in your best interest to say yes. From a personal growth perspective, it's as well in your best interest to say yes. Yes, allows you those moments to fight the fight with your team. Everyone wins. In those moments you are working toward a common goal with shared overlapping responsibilities with your team. Successful teams are built on a diversity of knowledge and experiences. When you're working on a common goal together on a time crunch the best comes out of each person. You'll learn more intimately how your colleagues approach issues.

Yes is where trust is built. I've said yes to projects I wasn't completely ready for. Yes, to take the lead on something I had never done before. Yes, to staying late when the team was running on fumes. And I don't regret one of those. Not because they were easy, because they were pivotal. They gave me the opportunity to show I could be counted on. Not just when things were smooth, but when things were hard. That's when people really start to notice. Yes, puts yourself in the room where the work is happening. And when you're in the room, you grow.

There's also something deeply personal about saying yes in the right moments. It signals to yourself that you're in. That you care. That you're not waiting for someone else to step up. And while yes should never be a default without thought, it should always be on the table when the mission matters and you know you can make a difference. There's a difference between being a people-pleaser and being a leader. Leaders say yes not because it's easy, but because it's aligned with who they want to be. If you feel that nudge, that internal voice confirming to yourself that you need to be part of this, trust it. That's not guilt. That's purpose tapping you on the shoulder. Say yes. Step up. You won't just contribute you'll transform.

Yes, With Intention: Don't Just Say it, Mean it

There's a difference between saying yes and meaning it. I've been on both sides of that statement. The side where I said yes out of obligation, and the side where I said it with purpose. The difference isn't always visible right away, but it always shows up in the outcome. A hollow yes is a placeholder. It fills the moment but not the need. An intentional yes carries weight. It tells people they can count on you. That you've thought about it, committed to it, and you're going to show up fully. When you say yes with intention, you shift from being agreeable to being dependable.

I've learned the hard way that an unintentional yes does more harm than good. You think you're helping in the moment, but what you're really doing is spreading yourself too thin or letting something slip through the cracks later. That creates frustration for you and for the people relying on you. But when your yes comes from clarity and commitment, it builds trust. It shows that your word means something, and people start to lean on you not just because you said yes, but because they know you meant it.

These days, I don't say yes until I'm sure I can follow through. And if I say it, I'm all in. Whether it's a project, a late night to meet a deadline, or supporting someone through a tough stretch, my yes comes with presence, not just permission. That's what leadership demands. Not more words, but more meaning behind them. If you're saying yes just to look like a team player but not showing up with the energy to back it up, it's a disservice to you and to the people you say it to. But when your yes is rooted in intention, people notice. They trust it. And over time, that becomes part of your leadership identity.

One of the practices I've adopted as a leader is to pause when I hear a yes that doesn't feel fully backed. If someone gives me a quick yes that sounds like a placeholder, I'll follow up with a simple, "Walk me through how you're planning to approach it." Not to challenge them, but to give them space to either affirm their intent or realize they might need support or clarification. It's not about catching someone out, it's about raising the bar for accountability. If someone can clearly articulate the steps, the time frame, and what they might need from others, I know we're aligned. But if the response is vague or hesitant, it gives us a chance to correct the course early before something slips. That one small follow-up turns a hollow yes into an intentional conversation and that's where real leadership happens.

The Yes-to-Growth Ratio, Finding Balance So You Don't Burn Out

There's a fine line between saying yes to grow and saying yes to the point of burnout. Throughout my career I believe I did this well. There are times I feel stretched, and I must work a bit more to succeed at something I added to my plate, but I learn quickly where my limit is, or was. I tried not to fully commit to yes being a door to opportunity, and the more doors I walked through, the faster I'd get where I wanted to go. Not always the case and dangerously close to burnout. I learned that too many yeses without intention will stretch you thin, and stretched too far, you break. I've hit that wall. I've said yes to everything to be helpful, to be seen, to not let anyone down and in the process, I started letting myself down. Saying yes should build something. When it starts tearing you apart, that's your signal.

The growth comes from yes, but the clarity comes from knowing which yeses matter. If every yes is equal, then none of them stand out. That's why I started being more selective. Not with a hard no, but with a thoughtful pause. Can I do this well? Will this grow me or drain me? Am I doing this because I want to, or because I feel like I must? Those are the questions that started shaping my yes-to-growth ratio. I don't say yes less, I say it smarter. I say it when I know I can be all in, not halfway there just to check a box. That mindset has changed how I lead and how I protect my energy. Consider a previous topic on allowing others to grow. Don't say yes to something you can do in your sleep, especially when it's a growth opportunity for others. Don't consume all the yes, leave some for others.

As a leader, I also watch for this in my team. The people who always say yes, who always jump in, who never push back, are the ones I check on the most. Because I know that path. I've walked it. I've worn the yes label until it became a weight. So now, I help my team navigate their yeses with intention. I remind them that saying yes to everything isn't leadership or task completion, it's exhaustion. Saying yes to the right things at the right time with the right focus, that's leadership. And that's where real, sustainable growth begins. If someone is telling me yes a lot, I will have a very meaningful conversation where I ask, "are you sure you can do this". Listen to the answer and ask more questions. Why are they stretching themselves, will other important work drop or be completed less effectively. Walk that line carefully. Allow them to say yes but as their leader ensure you're guiding them down the right yes path. The proverb "He who chases two rabbits catches neither" applies here and I use it as needed to highlight the point.

As I look back on my journey from delivering computers at Ericsson, to managing client accounts at Perot Systems, and adapting to global operations at Cadbury, I see a career shaped not just by roles and responsibilities, but by a slow and steady realization: I wanted to lead. For many years, I led people and projects without fully committing to leadership as a career. I was gaining experience, guiding teams, and managing outcomes, but I hadn't yet made the mental shift from "managing" to truly being a leader. It wasn't until I was midway through my time at Kraft that everything started to click.

I realized that leadership wasn't something I wanted to fall into, it was something I wanted to own. I immersed myself in leadership books, signed up for courses, and started studying the behaviors of leaders I admire. And something unexpected happened: everything I read, everything I learned, made sense. It didn't feel foreign or out of reach. It felt familiar. Like I had already been living parts of it, just without the intention or clarity behind it. That realization changed everything. It gave me confidence not just that I could be a strong leader, but that I already was. I just needed to lean into it.

The final piece was understanding what would help me grow even further. The answer wasn't a new title or a bigger team. It was a mindset shift. I needed to say yes more. Yes, to experiences I hadn't had. Yes, to challenges I wasn't sure I was ready for. Yes, to stepping into uncertainty with the belief that even if I didn't have the answer yet, I could figure it out. Saying yes became my way of building momentum. It pushed me into situations that refined my thinking, tested my resilience, and expanded my ability to lead.

That was the turning point. I committed not just to being in leadership, but to becoming the kind of leader others could count on, learn from, and grow with. And it started with that simple decision: to show up, to keep learning, and to say yes when it mattered most.

Lessons Learned

Leadership isn't a position you're given; it's a mindset you choose. For years, I was managing people and projects without fully embracing what it meant to lead. It took intentional learning, self-reflection, and a willingness to step into discomfort for me to realize that leadership is less about authority and more about accountability, growth, and service. The turning point came when I committed, not just to being in leadership, but to becoming a leader others could trust, learn from, and grow with.

Saying yes became a key part of that transformation. But I learned quickly that saying yes isn't just about being helpful, it's about being intentional. When the work is hard, when the team needs you, or when growth is on the line, saying yes with clarity and follow-through builds trust and credibility. It shows you care not just about the outcome, but about the people doing the work alongside you. Those are the yeses that build careers and reputations.

Still, a yes without meaning is just noise. One of the most important lessons I've learned is that intentional yeses distinguish dependable leaders from agreeable ones. A thoughtless yes can lead to disappointment, for you, your team, and the work itself. Leadership isn't built on convenience; it's built on consistency. And when your yes carries weight, people notice. They lean on it. They trust it.

At the same time, even the right yes can be overused. Saying yes to everything is a fast track to burnout, for yourself and for your team. Leadership also means knowing when to step back so others can step up. It's about creating space for growth, not consuming every opportunity yourself. Protect your yes so that when you give it, it carries the value and presence it deserves. That balance, that discipline, is what makes your yes one of the most powerful tools in your leadership toolkit.

Details Matter

Small Things are Big

I'm a detail-oriented person by nature but I wsn't early in my career. In fact, early in my career, I prided myself on being fast. Quicker than the next person. I moved quickly through tickets, cranked out emails, got through meetings with minimal notes if any, and checked off tasks like I was racing against time. It wasn't that I didn't care about quality, I just thought getting it done was more important than how it was done. But eventually, I started noticing something. The people who were consistently trusted with high-impact work weren't always the fastest. They were the ones who slowed down just enough to get it right. Not flashy. Not loud. Just steady, thorough, and respected.

One moment that changed my mindset happened during a team project where I had written up a documentation guide for a new system rollout. I was an individual contributor for a global company. We were making a change to a system that would cause users to have to work differently. When I completed it, I was proud of it, I understood it, and got it done ahead of schedule and felt good about it. A few days later, a colleague sent it back with what felt like an endless list of revisions. Typos. Missed steps. Formatting inconsistencies. Worst of all it didn't work that way for everyone, just me. I remember being frustrated at first. But once the frustration faded, what I really felt was embarrassment. I had been so focused on speed and delivery; I hadn't paid attention to the actual details. What hit me the hardest wasn't the corrections themselves, it was realizing I hadn't given the work the respect it deserved.

That was the beginning of a shift that to this day, more than a decade later, I started to care about the small things. Not just because I didn't want to be called out again, but because I realized the small things aren't small when you're leading. Had I been a leader and sent that out as it was the entire team would have been under fire for how bad it was. I also learned the hard way that not everyone is me. Everyone approaches doing things differently and no matter how much you think there's only one way to do something, there's more. A secondary lesson from that moment for me was that not only are people different, but your situations are too. Since this was an IT change it was even more complex in that not everyone had set up their system the same way or had the same version. Conscientious leaders show their commitment not just in what they do, but how they do it. The margin between good and great is often found in what others overlook. Proofreading that email one more time, testing the process end to end before rollout, double-checking your facts before you present. Over time, people start to notice that you care deeply, and that care becomes your credibility.

Credibility travels fast, and it can go in either direction. When you get the details right, people start to trust that your work is worth reading, following, and using. You become someone they can count on. But when you get it wrong, especially in ways that affect others, your reputation takes a hit that reaches further than you think. That document wasn't just for me it was for a global audience. And while I had good intentions, I hadn't considered how many people were depending on its accuracy. From that point forward, I stopped thinking of work as mine and started thinking of it as ours. Because when your work touches others, your name isn't just tied to the outcome it's tied to the experience they have because of it. That's where leadership shows up in the details.

Speed Without Precision is Risk

There's a natural drive in leadership to move fast and solve problems quickly, meet deadlines, keep momentum. But what I've learned is that speed without precision is a gamble. You might get something done quickly, but if it's wrong, confusing, or careless, the cost to fix it usually outweighs the time you saved. In leadership, your decisions and your deliverables ripple out to others. When you move fast but skip over key details, you're not just risking your own work, you're risking someone else's ability to do theirs effectively. It's a lesson I learned the hard way more than once, and it stuck.

In today's fast paced, microwave speed work culture, people are constantly pressed to make decisions on the spot. Emails are pouring in, Instant Messages won't stop, and you're in a meeting where the pace is fast. It's almost expected that you'll have the right answer immediately, even when the question deserves more thought. I've been in those moments, on a call, in a meeting, or even just passing in the hallway where someone asks for directions, and all eyes turn to you. The pressure to respond quickly can be overwhelming. But one of the most valuable habits I've learned is to pause. To say, "Let me think about that for a moment," or "I want to make sure I'm giving you the right guidance." That simple act of slowing down signals a maturity, not indecision. A quick answer that leads to the wrong action causes more chaos than taking an extra minute to provide a thoughtful one. As a leader, your job isn't just to react, it's to respond with clarity, and that often requires taking a breath before you speak. I've also found that not everything is urgent, it just sounds that way. If it's unclear just how hot something is, ask? I like to ask the return question "when is it due and why", "who needs it", and "what happens if that doesn't happen". Asking those questions will open a whole new world for you.

Precision isn't about being slow it's about being intentional. It means caring enough to double check, to ask clarifying questions, to take a breath before you hit send. Measure twice and cut once, always. Leaders who value precision don't just build better products they build better teams. Because when people know they can trust your attention to detail, they trust you more broadly. You won't be redoing work or explaining why it didn't turn out how it was intended the first time. The objective isn't to just be fast. The goal is to be right. And when can you deliver both? That's when your leadership starts to scale. I find somewhat sarcastic phrase fits here and I've used it, "anything worth doing once is worth doing twice".

Your Work Represents You

There's nothing more uncomfortable than being asked a question about your own work and not knowing the answer. I've been there. I've anecdotally heard, "don't ask a question you don't already know the answer to". More fittingly here it's "Never present something you don't know inside and out". The situation, you're presenting in a meeting, talking through a slide, and someone asks what the data means, or worse, challenges the math and you freeze. Not because you didn't care, but because you didn't double check. You assumed the numbers would speak for themselves. But they never do. If it's your slide, it's your story. It's your job to know what every figure represents and how you got there. Even if someone else pulled the data, if your name is on it, you own it. And when you own it, you need to anticipate the questions before they're asked. What does this trend tell us? Why does this chart stop in March? Where's the January data? What's the reason behind this spiking? These aren't curve balls or trick questions, they're table stakes.

Knowing your space means understanding more than just what's in front of you. It's knowing what came before, what's coming next, and how it all connects. I've seen many presentations that lead with numbers but not with purpose. Don't just show me a certain percentage increase, tell me what caused it. Was it seasonal? Was it a one-time event? And if it's down, why is it down? If you want to take things to the next level also have teed up how to fix or improve what's being presented. That's the next level. These are what gets missed the most. People present math but not meaning. Or they assume everyone else is tracking the background when the room is confused and too polite to ask. If you're going to speak about something, you need to live in it a bit. Walk the halls of the data. Ask yourself what your VP would ask. Ask what your team would ask. Challenge yourself before anyone else does. Also, if you are presenting something it's important that message can live on its own inside that presentation. Your work will move around, especially in a digital age. Ensure it makes sense to everyone without you there to present it.

And when it comes to delivering the message, don't forget to explain why the topic even matters. That's where credibility lives, in the clarity. I've sat through too many meetings where someone talks through metrics or updates and never once explains why we're even looking at them. Don't make your audience do the math or guess the takeaway. Show them that you've done the work. Knowing your space is about more than data, it's about owning the context, the implications, and the ripple effects. And when you can speak clearly, confidently, and with intention about what you're presenting, it doesn't just reflect well on you, it raises the bar for everyone around you. Don't force someone to say those dreaded words "why are we here". It's been said to me, and I've asked it of others. Get in front of that one by explaining why before you present anything.

Consistency Builds Reputation

Success leaves clues, it wants to be found. I've worked with people who always seemed to get it right. Clean deliverables, solid communication, always prepared in meetings. Early on, I assumed they were just wired differently. Smarter, more confident, more polished. What I came to realize is they weren't necessarily better, they were consistent. They found what worked, and they stuck with it. I started asking them how they did what they did. The more I asked, the more I realized I could adapt the structure, tweak it to fit my voice, and repeat it in my own work. Sometimes you don't have to ask, the evidence is right there in how they work, present, speak, etc. Paying attention to their consistency can't help but reveal what works for them. And you don't have to reinvent everything just be smart enough to learn from what's already working. And once you find your version of it, protect it and use it until it stops being effective. Like trying on clothes, sometimes they look good on the rack but not you. Find the shirt that fits .

Asking someone to review your work is not a sign you lack confidence. Some of the strongest deliverables I've ever presented went through two or three sets of eyes before leaving my hands. Not because I didn't know what I was doing but because I cared enough to make sure it landed right. Whether it's a presentation, a write-up, a roadmap, or a strategy. Being consistent doesn't just mean always doing it the same way. It means always doing it right. And part of doing it right is giving yourself the grace to pause, share, and ask, "Does this make sense to you?". The real leaders I trust are the ones who welcome feedback before it's too late to course correct. That's how you maintain quality without burning out trying to perfect everything solo. If I'm presenting to someone or a group for the first time, I'll ask others who have presented to them before for advice. Why wouldn't I!

We've all had moments when we finally figured out a method that clicks. A meeting cadence that runs smooth, a presentation style that feels natural, or a way of summarizing information that gets the point across fast. Once you find something that works, don't throw it away chasing something new just to be different. Stick with it. Polish it. Make it your standard. Consistency isn't boring, it's dependable. People start to notice that your work always has a clear narrative, your emails are always direct and informative, your status reports aren't filled with fluff. That kind of dependability builds trust. People won't wonder if you're going to hit or miss, they'll know what to expect. And that consistency starts to become your brand. The goal isn't to never change, it's to build habits that serve you until they don't. If you're going to change direction, change because there's a better way, not just because you get bored of your own system.

Every company has a style. Certain templates, reporting formats, communication expectations. You don't have to love every piece of it, but if you want to build a solid leadership reputation, you need to respect it. When your leaders or peers expect a certain kind of update, give it to them in the format they're used to. When your organization runs on visuals, don't send walls of text. If your leadership expects a three-bullet summary every Monday, don't try to impress them with a novel on Thursday. Being consistent with what your organization expects doesn't mean you're not being yourself, it means you understand the bigger system you're operating in. Leaders don't just lead people; they lead within a structure. And when you're fluent in that structure, people notice. They trust you to deliver, not just because you can, but because you do and you do on time, in the format they need, and with the reliability that puts them at ease. That's how reputations are built. Quietly. Day by day. Consistently.

Lessons Learned

The small things are never small, especially in leadership. Early in my career, I placed more value on speed than precision, but experience taught me that what gets overlooked often becomes what gets noticed the most just for the wrong reasons. One embarrassing moment of delivering a rushed and error filled document changed the way I approached every piece of work afterward. That mistake taught me that the quality of your work is a direct reflection of how seriously you take your role. And when others rely on that work, every typo, missing detail, or lack of context becomes a credibility gap that's hard to close once it's opened.

Over time, I learned that leadership isn't just about what you know, it's about how well you prepare, how clearly you communicate, and how much respect you give to the task at hand. Slowing down to get it right doesn't make you less efficient, it makes you trustworthy. Asking the right questions, reviewing your data, and being consistent in how you show up and deliver builds a reputation that extends well beyond one meeting or project. It's how people begin to trust your name when it appears on something because they know it's been done with care.

Most importantly, I learned that the work I do doesn't just represent me, it represents everyone it touches. Whether you're an individual contributor or a senior leader, your work creates ripple effects. And when those ripples are clean, clear, and intentional, you don't just lead tasks you lead culture. Attention to detail isn't perfectionism. It's ownership. And that ownership, over time, becomes your leadership signature.

Introduction To Evolve

Leadership isn't a finish line it's a constant evolution. The best leaders aren't the ones who have all the answers, they're the ones who keep growing, adapting, and learning through every season of their career. In this section, Evolve, we explore what it means to stay open to growth, even when you're already experienced. We'll look at how reflection fuels forward motion, how change challenges us to get better, and how embracing discomfort can lead to breakthroughs in both mindset and performance. Whether you're stepping into your first leadership role or looking to elevate how you lead others, evolution is the bridge between where you are and where you're capable of going. Leadership isn't static and neither should you be.

Leadership evolution often begins with clarity, the ability to see what no longer serves the mission and to reshape what comes next. When Steve Jobs returned to Apple in 1997, the company had become bloated and without direction. Dozens of product lines, a fractured brand identity, and no clear path forward. Many companies would have slowly restructured. Jobs radically simplified. He cut nearly all the products, refocused on design and user experience, and committed to excellence over volume.

Jobs's evolution as a leader didn't just come from bold moves, it came from relearning what mattered, shedding what didn't, and having the confidence to make hard decisions. He had failed before, publicly. But his return to Apple wasn't about revenge, it was about re-imagining. He evolved by letting go of what the company had become and returning it to its core: simplicity, creativity, and purpose. His story is a reminder that leadership isn't about holding on tightly, it's about knowing when to adapt and being bold enough to do it with vision.

Growth doesn't happen at all at once, it happens in layers. Sometimes it's slow and subtle. Other times it comes with a jolt that pulls you forward before you feel ready. But if there's one constant in leadership, it's this: you cannot stay still. You must evolve. The world around you will shift, your team will change, the business will expect more, and so will you. Leadership isn't about reaching a final form. It's about learning how to adapt, stretch, and say yes to what's next, even when it's unfamiliar.

My own evolution as a leader wasn't defined by a single role. It was defined by my willingness to keep growing beyond each one. After my time at Cadbury, which eventually became Kraft, through a company divestiture, I found myself at a crossroads. I had built a solid foundation in support and operations, but I felt something shifting. I wanted to explore new ways to contribute and new challenges to take on. That shift led me to a contract role at Microsoft, where I had the chance to observe one of the most mature and innovative tech environments in the world. Even as a contractor, I soaked in the pace, the culture, and the expectations. I was learning by watching how excellence operated on a scale.

From there, I was offered a role at JCPenney, setting up a new support team as part of their "Plan, Build, Run" model. It wasn't something I had done before. It was challenging, and at times uncomfortable, but I said yes. That yes opened the door to a new opportunity: a transition into a Security Engineering Manager position. I had always worked near IT security, understood it, respected it, but I had never been responsible for it. Now, it was mine to lead. That position became the most rewarding I'd had up to that point. I learned more than I could have imagined from my peers, from my team, and especially from my CISO and our CIO. They modeled leadership in a way that stuck with me, which was thoughtful, forward-thinking, and invested in the growth of others. I still carry those lessons with me.

That role sets the stage for the next step. I moved into a Director role in IT Infrastructure at Santander, a North American division of a global financial institution. For the first time, I was responsible for leading multiple teams and aligning our work to broader enterprise strategies. The scope was bigger, the expectations higher, and the pace faster. But I felt ready. It was another step in the journey, one that built on everything I had already learned, but demanded more from me in return. At Santander I had the fortune of once again learning from world class leadership.

Next, I transitioned to a role at IBM, supporting governance within one of their cloud teams. For someone who had always admired IBM's deep technical culture, this was a dream come true. The talent, the scale, the history, it all felt like a masterclass in global technology. But after some time, I found myself wanting more. I wanted a challenge that would stretch me beyond governance, beyond stability. I wanted ownership. That's when I accepted a role as Deputy CISO, a position that quickly evolved into CISO at Dovenmuehle, a mortgage subservicer deeply committed to delivering best-in-class solutions for its clients.

That move was a leap. A big one. But I took it because I was ready to evolve again. I loved security. I loved the complexity, the pace, and the responsibility. And I wanted to lead it at the highest level. In hindsight, I realized something important: I had developed a pattern. I was continuously accepting bigger, harder challenges. And once a structure was built and working, I felt the pull toward the next problem to solve. The next opportunity to learn and lead.

But none of that would've happened in isolation. My evolution wasn't fueled by ambition alone, it was powered by connection. Nearly every role I've taken, except for one, came through a prior relationship. Someone I had worked with before. Someone who recognized something in me. Someone who said, "I think you'd be great for this." I can't overstate how much those relationships have shaped my journey. My growth didn't happen in a vacuum, it happened because others saw my potential and gave me the opportunity to rise to it, often before I even saw it myself.

The section ahead reflects my perspective on what it truly means to evolve as a leader. It's not about chasing titles or waiting for permission. It's about choosing growth, staying uncomfortable, and refusing to settle. To evolve is to keep moving, keep learning, and keep stepping into roles that challenge who you are, so you can become who you're meant to be.

Make yourself replaceable

My First We're All Replaceable Moment

One of the most significant moments for me was when I was an individual contributor. I immediately felt like my job was in jeopardy and was extremely uncomfortable. It happened the day someone I thought was irreplaceable left Cadbury. I looked up to this person, they were efficient, technical, collaborated with others and had been with the company for what seemed like forever. Not only was this person no longer here, but they were also gone before I got a chance to say goodbye. It was one of those situations. I remember asking my manager why, what happened, what does this mean and more importantly I asked how we were going to keep going without them. I was really asking "Should we panic?" Without flinching he calmly laid out who would take over which responsibilities and then said something that's stayed with me ever since: "No one is that important that they can't be replaced." In that moment, I realized how ignorant I'd been and how true that statement was. We are all replaceable. That's not a threat, it's a truth. And once you understand that your behavior changes. It took me another two positions at other companies to not only recover from that moment but to adopt it. Up until that moment I just resigned to the fact that I'd work harder than everyone else and ensure that while I may not be replaceable, I'd be missed.

When I made that turn later in my career, instead of guarding knowledge, I started sharing it. Instead of building silos, I built people. What you need to do is work in a way that makes it easier for others to step in, not harder. That mindset isn't about minimizing your value, it's about maximizing the team's. And in doing so, you become even more valuable. I've carried that belief with me ever since, and it's shaped how I now choose to lead, how I mentor, and how I build teams that don't just rely on one person to succeed. I firmly believe that I can't move up until someone can move into my current role. I also strongly believe that if that moment happens where I and someone else can do that same role I should allow them the opportunity to take it since it would be a new experience for them. They'll certainly bring in new insights and carry the torch you passed to them. I can help them move onto something different and accept a new challenge.

As I started my new role at JCPenney, I was told by the hiring manager that someone on my new team had also applied for the same position but didn't get it. That could have created distance between us, but instead I pulled them aside and said, "If you still want this job, I'll help you get there." That wasn't just a gesture, it was a promise. Over time, they gained exposure to more of what leadership entailed, and ultimately decided it wasn't the path they wanted. But the opportunity was real. That's what matters. I didn't come into that role to hold onto the seat I came to lead and grow people, to create a cycle of development that doesn't stop with me. As it turned out, after being in that position a year I had been given the opportunity to move into a different role because of a similar situation. I took it, and it led me down a different path than I was currently on.

When you work that way, openly, collaboratively, with humility, you don't just get the job done. You build trust. You create bonds that outlast the task at hand. There's something powerful about going through the tough stuff together and coming out stronger on the other side. Those are the moments that turn coworkers into teammates, and teammates into future leaders.

Share What You Know, Before You're Asked

There's something powerful about sharing what you know before you're asked. It signals confidence, not ego and it sets a tone for the kind of team you want to be part of. I used to think that if I figured something out, it gave me an edge. That edge made me valuable. And in some ways, it did. But over time, I realized I was only as valuable as the people I brought along with me. If I was the only one who knew how to fix a recurring issue, I would become a bottleneck. At first, that felt like job security. Later, it started to feel like a limitation. If you are the only person who knows something, especially if it's significant, you can say goodbye to any personal time, and you'll keep getting interrupted at work. Consider how it feels when someone shares something with you without being prompted. Be that person.

I remember a moment when a newer teammate was struggling to find an issue in one of our systems. I watched them stumble for a bit, and my first instinct was to wait and see if they'd figure it out. But then I asked myself a better question, why was this still hard to find? Why hadn't I already created a quick guide, a shortcut, something they could use without having to ask? So, I made one. Simple, nothing fancy but it saved time for everyone moving forward. What took me fifteen minutes to create has probably saved hours for others since. That's the kind of work that doesn't show up on a to do list, but it builds trust in ways nothing else can. I personally don't like creating process documents. They can be so tediously detailed but there's nothing more valuable. Sharing knowledge with documentation and reinforcing with a live transition will build a significant amount of trust and respect.

When you freely share what you know, you create more capacity across the team. You stop being the only point of contact. People aren't waiting for you to answer something they could already know if you'd shared it earlier. And here's the other truth, it's not just for them. It's for you. Because the moment you start creating space for others to step up, you make room for yourself to move forward. The people who give away what they know are often the same ones trusted to take on more. Not because they hoarded the answers, but because they multiplied them.

I've seen careers stall because someone wanted to hold onto their niche, protect their knowledge, or stay "essential". But essential and irreplaceable are not the same thing. I don't want to be the only one who knows how to do the thing, I want to be the one who taught everyone how to do it better. That's leadership. That's how you build a legacy that lasts longer than any one person. And that starts by sharing before you're asked.

Build People, Not Dependence

Let's now look at this in practice. You're the go-to person. Everyone comes to you with questions, asks for your input, waits for your sign-off. At first, it feels good like a badge of honor. You're trusted, relied on, needed. But slowly, it starts to weigh on you. Every decision funnel through you, and your calendar's jammed with tasks that shouldn't all be yours. You're not just leading; you're carrying. And eventually, you realize what looks like strength is a form of dependence. The team isn't growing, they're leaning. Hard. And you're the crutch.

Imagine stepping into a meeting where your team looks at you for every answer, and instead of responding, you pause. You ask them what they think. You let the silence stretch. It feels uncomfortable at first, like you're letting something fall. But you're not. You're creating space for others to step in. And as they start offering input, taking ownership, making calls, you start leading differently. Not by doing, but by guiding. Not by controlling, but by coaching.

There will be missteps. Maybe someone makes a call you wouldn't have. Maybe a project hits a bump. But you resist the urge to take over. You offer feedback, you adjust, and you keep pushing ownership back into their hands. You'll start noticing changes when people come to you with updates, not just problems. Decisions get made without your constant involvement. The team starts to operate with a rhythm that doesn't rely on you to keep the beat.

That's when you've moved from building tasks to building people. And when your team succeeds without needing you in the center, that's not a loss of control. It's the proof you've led them well. The strongest teams aren't the ones that depend on their leader, they're the ones shaped by them and empowered to keep going long after the leader steps back. That's the goal. Not to be essential forever, but to lead in a way that creates independence, confidence, and future leadership in others.

Creating A Culture of Succession

Start small. Share your thinking behind key decisions. Let someone shadow you during high-level meetings. Hand off pieces of your responsibilities before you need to. Not to dump work, but to develop capability. The more exposure anyone can obtain on what's ahead, the more confident they become in their ability to step up. You're not just preparing a backup plan; you're creating a future leader. And that's how trust spreads throughout a team.

Another way is to give others visibility into the "why" behind your decisions. For instance, if you're putting together a strategy or making a call on priorities, pull a team member into that process. Talk through how you arrived at your conclusion. Let them see the factors you weighed and the risks you considered. They're not just learning the answer, they're learning how to think like a leader.

You can also build a succession culture through cross-training. Assign team members to teach others the work they specialize in, not only to back each other up, but to foster a mindset that knowledge is meant to be shared, not hoarded. It sends a clear message: we grow together. When your team starts to operate with that mentality of teaching, shadowing, documenting, and lifting one another, you're not just building skills, you're creating a system that can thrive even when people move on or move up. And when the opportunity arises, advocate for someone else's advancement even if it means they leave your team. That's succession in its truest form. It's not about holding people close, it's about pushing them forward, knowing that when you invest in their growth, you invest in the strength of the culture you're building.

A true culture of succession means no one hoards knowledge, and no one is afraid of being replaceable. In fact, being replaceable becomes the mark of great leadership. Because it means you've taught, empowered, and paved the way for others. You don't create succession by accident, you create it by being intentional, open, and committed to seeing your people rise. And when that's the culture, everyone grows.

Succession And the Master Plan in Action

When someone decides to leave your organization for a better opportunity, it can be bittersweet. On the one hand, you naturally want to retain great people. On the other, if you're leading with the right mindset, you see their success as part of your success. It's easy to fall into the trap of disappointment or even frustration when someone moves on, especially when they've been a key part of the team. But if you've built a culture of growth and succession, their departure isn't a loss, it's a milestone. It means they've developed, they're ready for the next step, and you played a role in helping them get there.

I remember one of the most impactful leadership moments I've personally experienced was when I left a company for a larger role. I was leaving JCPenney as a Manager, and I was taking a Director at Santander. The leader I reported to had taught me so much. How to think strategically, how to lead people with purpose, and how to navigate difficult decisions. When I told her I was leaving, I expected a conversation filled with mixed emotions. I certainly was already sad I was leaving. Instead, she congratulated me, pulled the team together, and gave me a warm and thoughtful send off. That moment left a lasting impression. She wasn't just a great leader because of how she led me, she was a great leader because she let me go with grace. Those are the proud moments, for you and for them. If you've led with intention, you've already been preparing others to step in. Let it happen. And when someone else's career takes off, celebrate it. You helped build that.

Lessons Learned

The idea of making yourself replaceable can feel uncomfortable at first. But in leadership, it's one of the most powerful and selfless principles you can adopt. When you build others up, share what you know, and actively prepare people to step into your shoes, you're not minimizing your value, you're multiplying your impact.

What I've learned over the years is that your goal isn't to be the only one who can do the job. It's to be the one who helps others learn how. That shift in thinking unlocks growth not just for the people around you, but for yourself too. It creates capacity on the team, builds leadership pipelines, and opens doors for new opportunities both for those you're mentoring and for yourself.

People will leave. Promotions will happen. Roles will evolve. But if you've led with a mindset of sharing knowledge, empowerment, and succession, you won't just be reacting to those changes you'll have helped build the foundation for them. That's the mark of real leadership. It's not in how much you carry, but in how well you prepare others to carry on without you.

Change with Change

The Next Two Chapters

As a leader, evolving isn't just about reacting to what's in front of you, it's about how you respond and who you become in the process. In this next part of the book, we'll explore two concepts that often get grouped together but serve different purposes. These two chapters are changing with change and being adaptable. One focuses on evolving with your environment, the external shifts in business, technology, or strategy. The other is about internal flexibility and how you personally respond when plans fall apart, or things move unexpectedly. These chapters are paired together because both are required for growth. One keeps you aligned with the world around you and the other keeps you balanced within it. Together, they help you lead through uncertainty with clarity and confidence.

The Company Grows, So Should You

When a company evolves, the people within it have two choices: grow with it, or get left behind. I learned this lesson firsthand during one of the most transformative stretches of my career. I was working for Cadbury Schweppes when its U.S. beverage business, which included Dr Pepper, was spun off in 2008 to form the Dr Pepper Snapple Group. Shortly after, in 2010, Cadbury now focused solely on confectionery and was acquired by Kraft Foods. That acquisition brought significant changes: new leadership, new systems, and new regions of the world now had a direct influence on how we worked. Just as I started to adapt to that structure, Kraft split in 2012 into two distinct companies, Mondelez International, focusing on global snacks and confectionery, and Kraft Foods Group, which retained the North American grocery business. Then in 2015, Kraft Foods Group merged with Heinz, forming The Kraft Heinz Company, one of the largest food and beverage companies in the world. I stayed with Kraft Foods Group in 2012 and left in 2015 during the Heinz merger. To say this was a learning experience is an understatement. It was a learning experience on so many levels.

Each of these transitions came with its own challenges, shifts in culture, and changing expectations. But with every change, I had the same choice, adapt or get left behind. I chose to grow. And in doing so, I discovered that staying within the same company doesn't mean standing still. In fact, the journey I had moving through roles, teams, and entirely new organizations without technically "leaving", taught me how to evolve within constant change.

Each phase brought a different set of expectations. Roles changed, organizational charts shifted, priorities were redefined. And yet, through all of that, one thing remained constant, the need to evolve personally if I wanted to stay relevant. That period taught me to lean into disruption rather than resist it. We talked previously about saying yes when you already know the answer must be yes. This was a prime example of that mentality. I knew what was happening and I needed to get on board. I had to learn new tools, navigate new leadership styles, adapt to changing strategies, and rebuild working relationships from scratch in some cases. But more than that, I had to change how I saw myself. I stopped clinging to what I used to do well and started asking what the company needed next and how I could grow into that version of myself.

As the scale of the company expanded, I quickly realized I couldn't hold onto everything I once owned so tightly. The scope was too big, the pace too fast, and the priorities too dynamic. I had to learn to give up control and to trust others to take on pieces of what I used to manage personally. That wasn't easy. Like many people, I felt the need to prove my value, especially in a new organizational structure where my reputation hadn't caught up to the change. But letting go of control didn't mean stepping back, it meant stepping up in a different way. I focused on enabling others while continuing to raise my hand for new opportunities. I said yes to global projects, cross-functional initiatives, and efforts that stretched me into new areas of the business. Each yes helped me evolve, even if it meant temporarily operating in the unknown. That's how I stayed visible, valuable, and growing by embracing change not just in theory, but in how I worked every day.

Change in a company isn't just structural, it's cultural. It shifts the expectations of what good leadership looks like. If the business is getting more global, more agile, more digital, then you need to be too. Staying still while the company moves forward means falling behind. But if you can read the signs and stay curious, these moments of transformation become some of your best opportunities to grow. They stretch your skills, challenge your assumptions, and make you a more well-rounded, future-ready leader.

What helped me immensely during those transitions was the groundwork I had already laid by showing up consistently, building trust, and collaborating well with others. That kind of reputation has a way of preceding you, especially when you're stepping into a new territory with unfamiliar leaders. I didn't have to start from scratch every time because the people who had worked with me before often spoke on my behalf. Whether it was a quick message to a new leader saying, "You're in good hands," or someone vouching for how I handle tough situations, that trust I had built became part of my leadership capital. It reminded me that how you show up today builds the bridges you'll walk across tomorrow. You're always building your story and others are always paying attention.

From Stability to Agility

There was a time when stability was the gold standard in business. Predictable processes, repeatable tasks, and long-term planning were the benchmarks of success. You knew what was expected, you did your part, and the machine kept moving. Leadership in those environments often meant maintaining the status quo, managing risk conservatively, and making incremental improvements over time. You're not always working on a conveyor belt, things change. Today, modern organizations are in a constant state of motion though new technology, shifting customer expectations, evolving workplace dynamics. The companies that thrive are the ones that prioritize agility, not just stability. And as leaders, we must shift with them.

Agility means being able to move quickly but thoughtfully. It means letting go of rigid plans and instead learning to navigate change with a clear head and a flexible approach. That's not always easy for those of us who built our careers on structure and predictability. I've felt discomfort myself when a multi-year roadmap was replaced with a rolling set of quarterly goals, or when what used to take six months now needs to happen in six weeks. But I've also seen how this kind of flexibility can spark innovation, uncover new strengths, and challenge people to lead in more dynamic, human ways. It pushes us to focus less on control and more on connections, reading the room, adjusting on the fly, and trusting our teams to adapt alongside us.

As a leader in today's business world, being agile doesn't mean having all the answers it means being ready to ask better questions, shift priorities when needed, and help others stay anchored in purpose even when the path changes. You become less about enforcing a plan and more about enabling progress. You start creating a culture where iteration is normal, feedback is constant, and experimentation is welcomed. And in doing so, you don't lose stability, you redefine it. Because in a fast-moving environment, the most stable thing you can offer is leadership that stays steady, not rigid. That's how you evolve with your company instead of being left behind by it.

What Got You Here Won't Necessarily Get You There

A good leadership lesson to learn is that what got you to your current role won't necessarily be what propels you into the next one. It feels counterintuitive at first and after all, your hard work, technical ability, attention to detail, and consistency likely played a big role in getting you noticed and promoted. But as you move up the expectations shift. It's no longer just about how well you execute it's about how well you enable others to execute. The hands-on work that once made you successful begins to take a back seat to influence, vision, and strategy. That transition is not automatic. It requires intention, self-awareness, and a willingness to evolve.

Early in your career, success might have been measured by how much you could personally accomplish in a day. But as a leader, your impact is measured by how well you can multiply that success across a team. That means letting go of being the subject matter expert in every room and instead becoming the person who builds the right rooms, asks the right questions, and empowers the right people. That evolution can be uncomfortable. There's a vulnerability in not being the one who knows all the answers anymore. But in that space is where leadership begins not by having the solution, but by guiding others to discover it.

Each new level of leadership asks something new from you. Sometimes it's learning to communicate more broadly, or to shift from reactive problem solving to proactive planning. Sometimes it develops emotional intelligence to navigate relationships with more empathy and patience. You must trade in old habits for new tools. The challenge is knowing which ones to keep and which ones to leave behind. What served you as an individual contributor may not be scaled as a leader. And what worked in a small team may not translate into a larger, more complex organization. But the leaders who thrive are the ones who keep refining, keep adjusting, and keep learning. They recognize that success isn't a destination, it's a continuous evolution.

Change is Emotional, Lead Through it Anyway

Change triggers emotion before it sparks logic. It's human nature that when something shifts, especially unexpectedly, our first reaction is often to feel rather than think. Uncertainty makes people anxious, loss of control can stir frustration, and the fear of being left behind or becoming irrelevant can creep in. As a leader, you don't get to skip those feelings. You do have a responsibility to manage them, both in yourself and in others. Because while emotions are real, if you let them take the wheel, they'll often drive you in the wrong direction. Leading through change doesn't mean pretending everything is fine. It means acknowledging discomfort, recognizing the emotional undercurrent, and choosing to lead with steadiness anyway.

In my own experience, especially during times of mergers and divestitures, I saw firsthand how emotional change can get. During the examples I gave at the beginning of this chapter with multiple mergers and divestitures. At first, I found myself frustrated. Roles changed, reporting lines shifted, priorities were constantly being rewritten. It felt like everything I had built could be undone overnight. But once I allowed myself to sit with that emotion and strip it down to what it really was, fear of losing relevance, fear of the unknown, I was able to think more clearly. I realized no amount of emotional reaction was going to stop the changes from happening. What could make a difference was how I responded, how I adapted, and how I helped others do the same.

The most important shift I made in those moments was to switch from reacting to leading. Recognize and put on hold the emotions and focus on the mechanics. Stick with what you know. I couldn't control the decisions being made above me, but I could control how I showed up for my team. I made it a point to be honest, to listen, and to provide stability even when I didn't have all the answers. I reminded myself and others that change, while uncomfortable, always brings opportunity and if we're willing to look for it. The truth is, if you try to wait until you "feel better" about change before acting, you'll often miss your window. Feelings can be loud, but leadership is built in the quiet space where logic meets intention. Recognize the emotion, respect it but don't let it lead you. Because if you want to evolve through change, you must choose to lead through it, even when it's hard. Especially then. The leaders around me did just that and it was because of them, and what I learned in those moments that helped me get through those uncertain times.

Making Change Part of the Culture

The best way to prepare for change is to stop treating it like an interruption. Instead of bracing for impact every time something shifts, build a team culture that expects and embraces change as part of how you operate. That means talking about it often, not just when it arrives. It means reinforcing that adaptability is a strength, not a reaction. When you normalize change, people stop resisting it and start looking for how they can grow through it.

Creating systems that support this mindset is key and sharing information early, encouraging cross-training, asking "what's next?" in team discussions. These aren't just habits, they're signals that evolution is part of the job, not a detour from it. When your team sees change as part of their rhythm, they become more confident, more resilient, and more ready for what's next. That's not just good leadership; it's building a future-ready culture.

Lessons Learned

Change is no longer the exception, it's the constant. One of the most impactful lessons I've learned as a leader is that your ability to grow must match the pace of the environment around you. Throughout periods of massive organizational shifts, mergers, and divestitures, I realized that simply doing what had always worked wasn't going to be enough. The moment you stop evolving, you start becoming irrelevant. Leading through change means more than just reacting, it requires conscious evolution. The key lesson: adapt with the company, not in response to it.

It also became clear that evolving as a leader meant giving up control to scale impact. As companies grow, so must your mindset. You can't lead the same way in a global, complex organization as you did in a smaller, local one. I learned to trust others, share ownership, and find value in enabling rather than owning. Saying yes to new opportunities even when I didn't feel fully ready kept me growing and helped others grow too.

Perhaps most importantly, I learned that emotional awareness during change is as critical as strategic agility. Change can be frustrating, confusing, and disorienting. But if you let emotion steer your behavior, you'll often miss the real opportunities that come with transition. Leadership in these moments isn't about avoiding discomfort it's about guiding yourself and your team through it with clarity and intention. When change becomes part of your culture, not just your crisis response, you lead with steadiness instead of stress. And in today's world, that might be the most valuable trait a leader can offer.

The Mistakes That Make You

There are two kinds of mistakes I've learned to pay attention to. The first is the one you know you made, the result of a bad decision, a rushed action, or something you should have handled differently. You feel it right away. It's uncomfortable, but it's also clear. You own it, learn from it, and move forward. The second kind is trickier, it's the mistake you don't recognize as a mistake in the moment. It's when you say something in a meeting that shuts someone down, or when you ignore a small issue that later turned into a big one. Those are harder to see because they often come from a blind spot. What I've learned is that leadership means being open to discovering those unseen mistakes and being willing to reflect and not just react. The visible mistakes shape you, but the invisible ones humble you. And it's in that humility that real growth begins.

Mistakes, whether big or small, are some of the most significant learning opportunities you'll ever get in your career. I didn't always see it that way. Early on, I thought mistakes were setbacks and something to avoid at all costs. But over time I realized they're moments of clarity, showing you exactly where you can grow. Sometimes they're obvious and tough, like missing a deadline or making the wrong call in a decision. Other times, they're smaller, more subtle like a conversation you could've handled with more empathy, or a detail you overlooked that created unnecessary stress for someone else. Those small moments may not feel like much at the time, but when you reflect on them, they become quiet teachers that help you fine-tune how you show up.

I've come to believe that mistakes are just course corrections in disguise. They guide you back to a better path if you're willing to look at them with honesty. The best leaders I've worked with didn't pretend they were perfect. They acknowledged where they could have done better and used those moments to improve not just for themselves, but for the people around them. That mindset shift changed how I approached my own growth. Now when I don't feel right about an action or decision I pause and ask, "What is this here to teach me?" Because every mistake carries a message. And when you listen to that message, it becomes a step forward, not a step back.

Once, as an IT Administrator I made a mistake that caused a portion of the company to come to a grinding halt. I accidentally deleted something that instantly caused our companies users to be kicked out of anything they were doing without the ability to log back in. It was one of those moments where you're confident of what you're about to do but when you do it you have a sick feeling you should not have. It was the first time I made a mistake of this significance. Not knowing at the time what else to do, I immediately informed my manager who reacted in a way that at the time took me by surprise. He instantly began assigning tasks to resolve the issue. Once it was resolved he asked me if I understood how I had made the mistake then sent me on my way. No yelling, not written up, not being fired. That retelling of this event took a few short moments. In real time it took hours.

This moment for me was one of the first times I truly learned what leadership was. I made a mistake. Not a career ending one, but the kind that's not only embarrassing but highlighted my carelessness. The kind that to this day reminds me that mistakes happen and when they do it's not about the mistake it's about recovery from it.

From Mistakes to Growth

I've always admired Phil Jackson's approach to leadership, not because of the championships, but because of the way he trusted his team to lead themselves. He was the kind of coach who didn't call a timeout every time things got difficult for his team on the court. He didn't jump in to fix everything. He believed in creating space for his players to figure it out on the floor. That kind of leadership takes patience. It takes confidence not just in yourself, but in the people around you. And it reminds me that sometimes the best thing you can do as a leader is step back, not step in. Pick these moments carefully of course. But when you can let others grind through an issue, let them grind. By doing so they learn how to resolve issues on their own or as part of a team. By learning this while in a true issue, in real-life problem-solving mode, it sinks in more. The experience sinks in more both if it's a success and if it results in a failure. Successes learnings come quickly; the failures however take time to sink in. Regardless, it's imperative that you give your team room to grow like this. It's important to do a post issue review. Drive home the right decisions and reinforce how the bad ones could have been better.

There's an instinct to want to control outcomes, especially when the pressure is high. I've felt it. That urge to jump in, give direction, solve the problem before it spirals. But what I've learned through experience and watching leaders like Phil Jackson is that stepping back doesn't mean you're doing nothing. It means you're giving people room to grow. You're saying, "I trust you to figure this out," and that kind of message builds more than skill. It builds belief. And that belief shows up later when the pressure's higher, the stakes are bigger, and the team doesn't panic because they've already learned how to lead themselves.

As a leader, you don't have to have all the answers. In fact, thinking you do can sometimes get in the way. Leadership is about creating the conditions for others to succeed even if that means watching them struggle a little. It's not easy. It takes self-awareness and restraint. But the long-term impact is powerful. You're not just leading a team you're building leaders within it. And that's the kind of leadership that lasts beyond the game.

There's a section I cover later making yourself obsolete. I'll go into more detail on that thought later but for now I want to highlight that your team needs to be successful without you. If you want to grow, if you want them to, and if you ever want to step away for a day off and trust your team can keep the ship afloat you must give them the room and opportunity to experience what that feels like without having a lifeline.

Finding the Mistakes You Can't See

This one took me a while to understand. There are mistakes you know you've made, and then there are the ones you don't even realize you're making. It wasn't until later in my career that I started to see the difference. I used to think if no one said anything, it meant I must be doing fine. But silence doesn't always mean success. Sometimes feedback never comes. Sometimes people don't feel comfortable speaking up, especially if you're in a leadership role. And that's how blind spots grow. I look back now and realize there were times I said the wrong thing, overlooked someone's contribution, or decided without enough input and I didn't know until months later. Or worse, not at all.

What I've learned is that you must go looking for those kinds of mistakes. You must create space for feedback, even when it's uncomfortable. Ask people you trust, "Is there anything I could be doing better?" Then stop talking and listen. I remember the first time I did that, someone told me I came off too strong in meetings and it shut down conversation. That was hard to hear. I talked about this earlier as something I work on. But it changed everything. I didn't fix it overnight, but that moment made me more aware. And that awareness made me a better communicator, a better teammate, and a better leader.

The lesson for me is this, just because you can't see it, doesn't mean it's not there. And just because no one's brought it up doesn't mean it doesn't matter. Real leadership is being willing to dig into things that aren't obvious. The quiet mistakes. The unintended impact. The patterns that only show up in hindsight. It's humbling, no doubt. But it's also powerful. Because when you start to uncover the things you couldn't see before, you grow in ways that go beyond your role. You become someone people trust more not because you're perfect, but because you care enough to look inward and grow outward.

One of the things I've had to learn over time is how important it is to be mindful of how others receive my message. It's not just about what I say, it's about how it lands with the person hearing it. I used to think if my intentions were good, that was enough. But I started noticing that some people responded well to my style, and others didn't. That's when I began to pay attention to how those same people reacted to other leaders. Some needed direct and to the point communication, others responded better to a softer, more collaborative tone. It made me realize that leadership isn't one size fits all. It's about reading the room, understanding your team, and adjusting your approach when needed. Being self-aware is part of it, but being others-aware is what makes you effective. When you take the time to understand how your message is being received, not just how it was delivered you become the kind of leader people want to hear from.

Mistakes Into a Leadership Style

When I first stepped into a leadership role, I thought communicating clearly meant saying things the way I understood them best. I focused on delivering the message how I would want to hear it directly, to the point, no fluff. At the core this is who I am so by leading this way I believed I was being genuine. I now know that I was being lazy. What I didn't realize at the time was that just because I was saying something clearly didn't mean people were receiving it clearly. I'd walk away from conversations thinking we were aligned, only to find out later there was confusion or disconnect. It took me a while to understand that communication isn't just about how you speak it's about how others hear you. And if the message isn't landing, that's on me to adjust, not to them to figure it out. That shift changed the way I approach conversation now.

I've been asked before what my leadership style is, and honestly, I don't have a simple answer. I don't subscribe to one fixed style or philosophy. What I've learned over the years is that leadership isn't about making people adapt to you, it's about you adapting to them. Every person, every team, every situation is different. What works with one person might completely be missed with another. So, I've stopped trying to lead one way. Instead, I try to listen, observe, and adjust. That's not being inconsistent, that's being intentional. It's knowing when to push and when to pull, when to speak up and when to listen. That flexibility is what's helped me build trust and get results.

I also don't see myself as a blueprint of one leader or another. I've worked with great leaders who showed me what to strive for, and I've worked with difficult ones who taught me what to avoid. I also recognize that just because I found those leaders either great or difficult I may not have understood them. Regardless I'm a firm believer that whether good or bad, great or difficult, mistake or success, there's a nugget of wisdom to be pulled somewhere. Both experiences shaped me. I've taken pieces from each of them and how they handled pressure, how they communicated, how they treated people and made something of my own. I'm not a copy of anyone else. I'm a collection of lessons. And I think that's what leadership really is. It's learning from the people around you, taking what works, leaving what doesn't, and never being too proud to adjust.

The moment you think you've got it all figured out is the moment you stop growing. And leadership, at its core, is about growth. Yours, and the people around you.

Lessons Learned

What I've learned through experience, sometimes painfully, is that mistakes are some of the most valuable leadership tools we have. The obvious ones teach you responsibility and resilience. The hidden ones are the ones that shape your awareness and humility. I used to think leadership meant having the answers and doing things right the first time. But real leadership is knowing that you'll get it wrong sometimes and being open enough to learn from it when you do. Whether it's a technical error that brings systems down or a poorly delivered message that leaves someone confused, the mistake isn't the end, it's the beginning of better.

The key is reflection. It's asking what the mistake is here to teach you. And it's creating space for others to do the same. When you give your team room to solve problems even when they stumble, you're building more than skills. You're building leaders. I've come to believe that growth isn't about perfection, it's about course correction. That means embracing mistakes as feedback, not failure. That means adjusting your message, your approach, and your mindset when something doesn't land. And most of all, it means staying humble enough to keep learning. Because leadership isn't a fixed style it's a collection of lessons, shaped over time, by every win, every miss, and every moment in between.

Be Adaptable

Control the Controllable

I learned a valuable lesson from my CIO at JCPenney. I was a manager at the time, still finding my footing, and figuring out where I fit in the broader leadership landscape. She said something that's stuck with me. It was that a good leader can lead any team. To her it wasn't about what you know, it's about how you lead. At first, I wasn't sure I agreed. I mean, shouldn't a leader understand the subject matter? Shouldn't they be technical experts to guide a technical team? But as I sat with it, I realized what she meant. Leadership isn't about having all the answers, it's about showing up with clarity, and consistency, especially when the answers aren't clear. It was a pivotal moment for me. That mindset changed the way I approached almost everything after that. I had been learning leadership lessons throughout my career about how to be a good leader. Reflecting on lessons, it was never industry or technology specific. Then why can't a good leader lead any team?

When you focus on the things you can control and how you lead, how you communicate, how you treat people, you free yourself from the anxiety of needing to know it all. That's the mistake I see a lot of new leaders make. They scramble to master every technical detail, to be the smartest person in the room, thinking that's how credibility is built. But the truth is, credibility is built through reliability. Through how you carry yourself when the pressure is on. Through your ability to stay grounded when things shift. I would hate having a team full of myself in the same room. Just imagine, all of them giving the same answers and constantly agreeing with me. No thank you. I want a room full of different thinkers and smarter people. I'm much happier leading smart people than trying to be the smartest.

There will always be things outside your control, the market changes, budgets get cut, reorganizations happen, technology evolves faster than training can keep up. You can't stop those waves from coming, but you can decide how you respond to them. You can be the kind of leader who brings focus into the middle of noise. And helps the team find the path when the map changes. That's what it means to control the controllables. You don't need to know everything about the work to lead the people to do it. What you need is the presence to keep the team steady, the mindset to stay teachable, and the consistency that builds trust even in the unknown. That's what scales. That's what stays around for the long term.

Change Your Plans, Not Your Standards

Plans will change, but your standards shouldn't. It's tempting in moments of disruption to loosen the grip on expectations just to get something across the finish line. But if you're not careful, you start making exceptions so often that you forget what the rule even was. As a leader, your team looks to you not just for direction, but for consistency. And consistency doesn't mean the path never changes, it means the commitment to how you work doesn't waiver, even when the path does.

I've been in more than a few situations where a strategy was fully mapped out, deadlines set, resources aligned and then something changed. New leadership, shifting priorities, a tool that didn't work the way we thought it would. In those moments, it's easy to let frustration lead. To lower the bar just to get through it. But that short-term gain almost always shows up later as long-term regret. I've learned to pause, reset the plan, and commit to the standard. You might deliver something later, or differently, but it still needs to be right. The quality, the clarity, the care behind the work, those things can't drop just because the situation has got hard.

A project I was once on shifted gears midstream. This was during COVID. Suddenly everyone is at home, everyone is remote, implement a solution that keeps people working and make it happen for all the users in the company. This was one of those moments where being in IT meant the entire company was looking at you to solve a problem, quickly. The pressure to just get it done was real. But instead of pushing out something half-baked, the team, through support and great leadership at the top, and a lot of hard work, got the job done. And we got it done in half the time we had been given, and that time was already cut in half. We asked, what were the things that we had to do, no matter how much the timeline flexed? That conversation gave us clarity. We refined the scope, poured ideas and hard work into it, and did not sacrifice quality. We realigned the plan without compromising the standards. And in the end, what we delivered was not only on time, but it also stood the test of time and remained the ongoing solution well through the COVID lockdown.

That's what leadership requires in fast moving environments. Agility in the how, firmness in the why. You may need to pivot, adapt, or even rebuild. But what does the standard of good looks like? That stays. Changing the plan doesn't mean changing your integrity. It doesn't mean changing your care for the details, your accountability, or your follow-through. Those are the things that define your leadership, not when it's easy, but when it would've been easy to let them slip.

Slow Down to Move Forward

There's a point in every leader's journey where speed feels like progress. The faster you move, the more you check off the list, the more productive you feel. But real leadership isn't about how fast you move it's about how intentionally you move. The truth is that, speed without direction is just motion. And motion in the wrong direction creates rework, confusion, and missed opportunities. Slowing down doesn't mean falling behind. It means taking the time to understand what you're doing and why it matters before charging ahead.

You'll face pressure to act quickly with tight deadlines, urgent meetings, unexpected pivots. But the leaders who thrive in those moments are the ones who pause long enough to get aligned. Ask yourself, Do I fully understand the goal? Have I clarified expectations? Is everyone on the same page? That extra moment of clarity on the front end often saves days or weeks on the back end. The pause doesn't delay progress, instead it accelerates it by eliminating avoidable mistakes.

As a leader, slowing down can be a sign of strength, not hesitation. When you see someone lost in thought, quiet, still, eyes fixed on something invisible, they're not stuck, they're thinking. Thinking may not look like doing, but it's often where real work begins. It tells your team you value precision, not just speed. It creates space for questions to be asked, assumptions to be challenged, and smarter decisions to be made. Teams feel more confident when they see their leader creating room to think. You set the tone that if you're steady, your team will follow suit. And when it's time to move, you'll all move faster because you're grounded in the same direction.

Leadership isn't about racing to the finish line, it's about ensuring you're on the right course. Take the time to slow down and assess before reacting. When you do, you'll find that forward momentum becomes more focused, more effective, and far more sustainable. Sometimes the most strategic step isn't a leap, it's a pause.

Thrive In the Grey

In leadership, not everything is black and white. In fact, most things aren't. The further you go, the more you'll find yourself operating in the grey. It's the space where the rules aren't clearly defined, where the data isn't conclusive, and where the decisions don't have one obvious answer. That's where real leadership is tested. Anyone can follow a checklist or manage by policy. But thriving in the grey requires judgment, emotional intelligence, and the confidence to make a call even when all the lights aren't green.

You will be asked to weigh competing priorities, resolve ambiguity, and move forward with limited information. It can feel uncomfortable at first, especially if you're someone who's used to certainty. But over time, that discomfort becomes an advantage and because most people avoid the grey. They wait. They hesitate. Leaders don't. Leaders step in, assess the landscape, and provide direction. Even if it's not perfect, movement in the right direction often matters more than waiting for the perfect plan.

What separates those who survive in ambiguity from those who thrive in it is a mindset shift. It's understood that clarity isn't always found, it's created. You ask better questions. You seek diverse perspectives. You build alignment not by having all the answers, but by guiding others through the uncertainty with calm and consistency. People won't always remember the exact decision you made but they'll remember how you made them feel during uncertain times. That's how trust is built in the grey.

If you're waiting for everything to make sense before you act, you'll miss your moment. Grey is where growth lives. It's where the decisions with the most impact are made. So, get comfortable with being uncomfortable. Get used to asking "What's the right next step?" instead of "What's the perfect solution?" And know that the more you lead through uncertainty, the more you build resilience not just for yourself, but for the people following you. Because when others freeze in ambiguity, great leaders move with purpose.

Outgrow The Comfort Zone

The comfort zone can feel like a safe place but stay in it too long, and it becomes a trap. It's where progress quietly stalls. Work becomes routine, the growth flattens, and before you know it, you're just going through the motions. That's exactly what happened to me. I was stuck in my career for about a year, showing up, doing the job, but feeling lost and without direction. I wasn't challenged, and more importantly, I wasn't challenging myself. Looking back, I didn't just hit a plateau, I had parked there. I had basically given up. In the moment I was there, it was after looking back that I realized how far into the comfort zone of the unknown I had got.

During that time, I gave my manager a tough run. I was difficult, disengaged, and didn't make it easy for him to support me. But he stayed consistent. He kept giving me space and opportunities even when I didn't recognize them for what they were. Years later, with more perspective and experience, I reached out to him to say two things. I told him thank you, and I'm sorry. He had been a good leader. I had been a bad employee. And that realization stuck with me. It taught me that being in a slump isn't just hard on you it can weigh on the people trying to help you too. Leadership requires grace not just for others, but for yourself as you learn.

Outgrowing the comfort zone often starts with a wake-up call, sometimes subtle, sometimes loud. It might come from a missed opportunity, a difficult conversation, or simply the nagging feeling that you're capable of more than you're doing right now. The key is not to ignore that feeling. Sit with it. Let it prompt you to ask better questions: What's next? What scares me? What am I avoiding? Growth begins the moment you stop settling.

Choosing to stretch yourself even when it's uncomfortable unlocks something powerful. It rewires your thinking and reframes how you see obstacles. Instead of asking, "Can I do this?" you begin to ask, "What will I learn by trying?" That shift fuels momentum. And the more you stretch, the more capacity you build for leadership, for empathy, for influence. Comfort might feel safe, but it won't get you where you're meant to go. The decision to outgrow it, is the first step toward becoming the leader your team and your future deserves.

Growth Looks Different Than You Think

Growth doesn't always look like a promotion or a new title. Sometimes it looks like staying in the same role but handling it with more confidence, more strategy, and more influence. It might look like having a tough conversation you would've avoided a year ago or stepping back to let someone else lead when your instinct was to take over. Growth often hides in the small shifts in how you react under pressure, how you give feedback, how you manage your energy. It's not always loud or visible. In fact, the most meaningful growth usually happens quietly, in the background, where you're learning, adjusting, and strengthening your foundation.

It's easy to miss your own progress when you're only looking for big milestones. But real leadership growth is layered. It's when you start asking better questions, showing up more consistently, or mentoring someone without being asked. If you don't pause to recognize those moments, you might convince yourself you're stuck when you're evolving. Give yourself credit for the progress that doesn't show up on paper. Because growth isn't always a new position, it's becoming someone more capable and self-aware than you were the day before.

Lessons Learned

Adaptability isn't a bonus trait in leadership, it's essential. The lessons throughout this chapter reinforce that success doesn't come from resisting change, it comes from responding to it with clarity and consistency. You don't need to control every detail, but you do need to control how you lead through the unknown. Whether it's a shift in plans, a new environment, or ambiguity creeping in, your ability to stay grounded while everything moves around you defines your impact.

This chapter also emphasized that adaptability isn't about lowering your standards. It's about adjusting your path while keeping your integrity intact. When you slow down, even briefly, to align on what matters, you accelerate progress. And when you choose to lead through grey areas rather than freeze in them, you build a reputation of calm in the chaos. Most of all, adaptability requires humility. To learn. To let go. To grow. It's what turns a good leader into a resilient one. One who outgrows comfort, thrives in uncertainty, and makes progress even when the map changes.

Strategies

Chapter Introduction

As you evolve in your leadership journey, one thing becomes increasingly clear, growth doesn't happen by accident. It takes awareness, effort, and, most importantly, strategy. This chapter outlines a collection of key strategies that have helped shape my own path as a leader. They're practical, repeatable approaches that I've seen work in real environments, with real people, under real pressure.

These strategies are about mindset as much as they are about execution. They'll help you think broader, act with intention, and lead with the kind of steadiness that others can rely on. You won't master them all at once, but even small, consistent progress in any one of these areas will move you forward. Leadership isn't about having all the answers, it's about continuously learning how to ask better questions and make better decisions. The strategies in this chapter are meant to help you do just that.

Start Now

If you never start, you'll never finish. Progress doesn't happen by waiting for the perfect plan, the perfect time, or the perfect confidence level. At some point, you must decide to move. I often use the analogy of pushing a snowball down a hill. At first, it's small, and it takes effort to get it going. But once it starts rolling, it builds momentum and grows. Occasionally, you might need to give it another push, steer it a little, or knock off the pieces that don't belong, but it's moving. And once it's moving, so are you. Leadership, like progress, starts with the decision to start. Don't wait. Push the snowball.

Pay Attention to Your Experiences

Paying attention to your experiences worked for me. Watching others succeed and adapting what I saw to who I was becoming. I consider myself lucky to have had every job I've held. Truly. All the struggles, successes, and relationships. The fact that someone chose me out of all the other candidates isn't something I take for granted. That feeling of being selected for a role, of being trusted to show up and contribute is something I continue to carry with me. But what I've come to realize over time is that gratitude and ambition don't have to compete. You can be happy where you are, while quietly preparing yourself for what's next.

Preparing To Be Ready

Being ready for the next opportunity starts with how well you show up for the one you already have. At one of my earliest jobs washing dishes in a small restaurant, I didn't know anything about career paths or growth frameworks, but I knew I wanted to do more. I focused on doing the job in front of me exceptionally well. I showed up early, stayed ready, and offered help before it was asked. I wasn't chasing the next role; I was preparing for it. That mindset still holds true in leadership. You don't wait for opportunity; you earn it by consistently performing with excellence and staying close to the work you want to grow into. Be present and be prepared. When the next role opens, it should feel less like a leap and more like a natural step forward.

Control What You Can Control

Being ready for what's next isn't just about big moves, it's about mastering the small ones you repeat every day. Most of us follow routines, and within those routines is a pattern of preparation or neglect. If you want to lead well and evolve as a professional, start by building habits that put you in control before the day takes it from you. Whether it's waking up early, reviewing your calendar the night before, or setting your intentions before emails flood in, those moments set the tone. You can't control everything, but you can control how ready you are. The leaders who thrive aren't reactive, they're prepared. They know their mornings matter, their mindset matters, and how they show up matters. Readiness starts in routine. When you build systems that support your day before it begins, you're already ahead.

Do You Really Need to Ask That Question

One of the simplest leadership strategies that often gets overlooked is learning when not to ask a question. Ask yourself this, if your boss wasn't around, what would you do? Do that. That's what being a self-led, trusted leader looks like. I often share this example, when you were a kid and you had to ask an adult if you should do something, it was usually because deep down, you already knew you shouldn't. The same principle still applies. If you know something needs to be done, do it. Don't wait for permission to do the right thing. A lot of the time, we ask not because we need direction, but because we want validation or visibility. Instead of asking, "Should I do this?" ask yourself, "Is this the right move?" If it is, own it. And when it's done, then communicate it. "Here's what I did and why." That's the difference between asking for permission and leading like you already know where you're going.

Be a People Person

Don't lead people without first trying to understand them as people. That doesn't mean prying into their personal lives or crossing boundaries they haven't invited you into. It means showing interest in who they are beyond their job title. Ask about their hobbies, what they enjoy outside of work, how they like to unwind. These questions may seem small, but they open the door to trust and connection. As much as I value my own experiences, I've learned to appreciate and learn from the unique paths and passions of others just as much. The better you understand what makes someone tick, the better you'll lead them. And when people feel seen as individuals, not just as employees, they bring more of themselves to work.

Manager vs. Leader

The difference between a manager and a leader often comes down to mindset and impact. A manager ensures things get done, they organize tasks, follow processes, and keep the team on schedule. A leader, on the other hand, inspires movement in the right direction. They don't just manage tasks; they also develop people. Managers focus on outcomes; leaders focus on growth. While good managers are necessary for operational success, great leaders create environments where people thrive, take ownership, and exceed expectations. A manager tells you what needs to be done. A leader shows you why it matters and empowers you to do it better. You need to be both a manager and a leader.

From Micromanagement to Disappearing

One of the most challenging transitions for a new manager is learning how to walk the tightrope between micromanaging and disappearing. Early on, it's natural to stay close to the work being done and to be in the trenches with your team, asking questions, checking on progress, and making sure nothing falls through the cracks. That level of engagement can help you build trust and show you're invested. But the key is not to stay there. As your team begins to operate more cohesively, your role shifts. Gradually, you pull back, not because you're less involved, but because you're building their confidence and autonomy. You move from directing every step to clearing the path. From checking every detail to being available for guidance. Leadership is less about hovering and more about knowing when to lean in and when to step back. Done right, the team won't feel abandoned, they'll feel empowered.

Leading in Every Direction, Up and Out

Great leadership isn't just about managing down it's about leading in every direction: up, out, and across. Leading up means keeping your leaders informed, anticipating their questions, and giving them confidence in your ability to handle your scope. Don't wait to be asked, communicate proactively, bring solutions, and share progress. Leading out means building strong partnerships with other teams and departments. The wider your awareness, the better your decisions. Great leaders don't lead in isolation, they connect dots, bridge gaps, and make sure their team's work aligns with broader goals. The most effective leaders are those who understand the whole playing field, not just their corner of it.

You Can Be Better

Believing in yourself is essential in leadership and it's just as important to remember that you're not flawless. Confidence without humility turns into ego, and ego is blind to growth. You can be capable, experienced, and still have blind spots. We all do. The key is to stay open to feedback, to surround yourself with people who think differently, and to constantly reflect on how you can improve. True belief in yourself isn't about thinking you're perfect, it's about knowing you're willing to keep learning, adjusting, and becoming a better version of the leader you are today.

Think Differently

Thinking differently is a leadership skill that separates problem solvers from problem dwellers. A leader once shared with me a mindset that stuck, "How would we do this if the way we do it now wasn't available?" That question flips your perspective. It removes the crutch of habit and forces creativity. It's easy to keep repeating what works, but true innovation comes when you imagine what's possible without the constraints of what's familiar. Great leaders don't just optimize the current path, they ask if there's a better one, and sometimes that means stepping off the trail completely.

Keep Learning Your Space

Personal growth as a leader starts with staying deeply connected to the space that you're in. That means continuing to learn not just about your craft or your team, but about your company, your industry, and the challenges and opportunities around you. Too often, people settle once they feel confident in their role, but leadership isn't a place you arrive at, it's a place you keep evolving within. The more you understand the environment you operate in, the more valuable your insights become. Keep asking questions, stay curious, attend that session, read that update, listen to your peers. When you keep learning your space, you don't just grow, you position yourself to help others grow too.

Own The Statements

Never reference statistics or reports you haven't read or don't fully understand. It's tempting to repeat numbers you've heard in meetings or pull a line from a report to strengthen your point, but if you can't explain the source or context, you lose credibility the moment someone asks a follow-up question. As a leader, your words carry weight, use them carefully. If data supports your case, that's great but not good enough. Make sure you've seen it, understood it, and can speak to it confidently. Quoting blindly isn't leadership, it's noise. And when you're in a position of influence, that kind of noise can create confusion, not clarity.

Connect With Like Minded People

Build or join a peer group where you can share ideas, ask for advice, and hear how others approach similar challenges. Leadership can feel isolated at times, especially when you're making tough decisions or navigating new territory. Having a trusted circle of peers gives you a safe space to think out loud, test your assumptions, and gain perspectives you might not have considered. It's not about having all the answers, it's about surrounding yourself with people who help you ask better questions. Whether it's a formal leadership roundtable or an informal group of colleagues you respect, find that circle and contribute to it often. It's not just support, its strategic insight, growth, and accountability all wrapped into one.

Know it's Yes Before You Ask

When you're preparing to ask for something like a budget increase, headcount, a new initiative, don't walk into the room cold. Preparation goes beyond knowing your numbers or building a solid case. It's about building alignment ahead of time. If possible, meet individually with each decision maker before the big ask. Understand their perspective, their concerns, and what success looks like to them. These conversations give you the chance to adjust your approach, refine your message, and most importantly, avoid surprises in the room. When people feel heard beforehand, they're more likely to support you in the moment. Big asks land better when they're not the first time your audience is hearing them. Set the stage, build the buy-in early, and turn a big request into an easy yes.

Keep Your Team Thinking

One of the most valuable things you can do as a leader is keep your team thinking. Not just doing but thinking. Ask engaging, open-ended questions that invite perspective, creativity, and challenge. Don't just ask for status updates, ask what's working, what's not, and what they would change if they could. Then actually listen. The goal isn't to have all the answers, it's to create space where ideas surface, problems get exposed early, and people feel seen for more than just output. When your team knows you're genuinely interested in how they think, they'll start thinking more critically, more confidently, and more collaboratively. That's where innovation starts. Not with a directive, but with a good question and a leader who's ready to hear the answer.

Us, Not I

As a leader, your language shapes your culture. One of the simplest but most impactful shifts you can make is replacing "I" with "us." Leadership isn't about personal credit; it's about collective success. When something goes well, don't say "I did this," say "we did this." Give credit to the people who made it happen, especially when no one's watching. That kind of humility builds trust and loyalty. People will work harder for a leader who sees their contributions and shines a light on them, not one who steps in front of it. The more you make it about the team, the more the team will make it about the mission. Great leaders don't seek the spotlight, they reflect it.

Office Politics

As a leader, it's important to understand the dynamics of your organization but there's a fine line between awareness and participation. You should absolutely listen, observe, and stay in tune with the tone of the team. Know what's being said in the halls, in the chats, and between meetings. That insight gives you a pulse check on morale, concerns, and culture. But engaging in gossip or adding to internal politics erodes your credibility. Be the person who listens without fueling the fire. Keep your focus on facts, solutions, and moving things forward. When people see that you don't take sides or feed the rumor mill, they'll respect your steadiness. That's how you stay in the loop without getting tangled in it.

Giving Others the Benefit of the Doubt

As a leader, one of the most human things you can do is give people the benefit of doubt. Not every off moment reflects laziness or lack of care, sometimes it's just a bad day, stress at home, or someone silently struggling. Instead of jumping to conclusions or assigning blame, pause and create space. If someone's energy is off or their work isn't quite what it usually is, assume grace before you assume the worst. And if the behavior continues, don't ignore it, ask. Not in a way that puts them on the spot, but with genuine care: "I've noticed you've seemed a little off, is there anything I can do to help?" That kind of leadership builds trust and reminds your team that they're seen as people first.

Communication
Communication isn't just about what you say, it's about how often, how clearly, and through what channels you say it. As a leader, you can't assume that one message in one format is enough. People absorb information differently. Some connect with a visual, others with a conversation, and some need to hear it more than once before it sinks in. That's why consistency and creativity matter. Say it in a meeting, follow up in an email, reinforce it in a 1:1. Use slides, stories, examples, whatever it takes. The goal is alignment, not just announcement. When your team knows you'll communicate regularly and in ways that meet them where they are, they're more likely to stay informed, engaged, and aligned to the bigger picture.

Use Clear Language
Clear language builds trust. As a leader, your credibility depends on how clearly you communicate, not how many buzzwords you use. Overusing filler phrases like "hey," or constantly asking and answering your own questions like "Are we aligned? Yes. Can we deliver? Yes.", can dilute your message and confuse your audience. Trendy terms like synergy or value-add may sound impressive but often lack substance. Speak plainly and with purpose. If you can't explain something simply, you may not understand it well enough. Clear, direct communication helps your team focus, respond, and act, and that's the foundation of any successful strategy.

Pause During Emotion
In leadership and in life how you react in the moment can shape your entire path. Emotions run high sometimes, especially when you care deeply about your work or feel misunderstood. But reacting too quickly can create consequences you can't take back. I learned this firsthand when I once rage quit after receiving a performance review that, while good, didn't meet the expectations I had set for myself. In the heat of the moment, I let frustration win. Thankfully, my boss had the wisdom to tell me to take a day and think about it. I did. I came back, retracted my resignation, and stayed the course. That decision ended up shaping one of the most rewarding chapters of my career. The lesson? Don't act on emotion, step back, cool off, and look at the full picture. A short pause can protect long-term progress.

Have Fun
Work takes up a significant portion of your life so why would you spend it without enjoying it? As a leader, it's not only OK to enjoy the journey, its necessary. Bring the energy that you want others to feel. Laugh when it's time to laugh, smile often, and find joy even in the pressure. Appropriate fun isn't a distraction, it's fuel. People work better when they're happy, not angry. They're more creative, more collaborative, and more

resilient. And so are you. A positive environment doesn't just make the day better, it makes the outcomes better. If you can't enjoy the process, you'll burn out before you reach the result. So, lead with a little lightness. Take the work seriously, but not yourself. It changes everything.

Knowing When to Stop

One of the most underrated leadership skills is knowing when to stop. Whether you're explaining an idea, making a case, or pitching a new initiative, if you see the light go on in someone's eyes, stop. If they've said yes, don't keep selling. You risk talking them out of something they've already agreed to. Read the room, recognize the moment, and move on. It's a balance of confidence and restraint. And speaking of knowing when to stop, I have more strategies I could share here but this chapter's gotten long enough. I'll practice what I'm suggesting and stop here.

Closing
Closing Summary

Leadership is not a title, it's a mindset, a commitment, and a practice. It's built day by day through awareness, strengthened by conscientious effort, and elevated through evolution. In Awareness, we explored the importance of being present, reading the room, and recognizing that every word, every action, and every moment matters. Awareness is the root of trust, it's how people know you see them, hear them, and value what they bring.

Conscientiousness reminded us that leadership is about more than hard work, it's about intentionality, integrity, and consistency. It's in the details, in how you follow through, and in how you make others feel through your effort. It's not always visible, but over time, it becomes the reputation you carry, and the foundation others lean on.

And in Evolve, we looked at growth not as a goal, but as a way of being. Leadership is not static, it demands change, self-reflection, and the courage to step into challenges that stretch you. Each career chapter, each new role, and each leap of faith becomes part of your evolution. It's how you move from manager to leader, from contributor to builder, and from learning to leading others through their own transformation.

If this book leaves you with anything, let it be this: Pay attention. Work hard. Keep growing. Say yes to the things that matter, even when they're uncomfortable. Lead with care, follow through with integrity, and never stop learning. Do that consistently, and you won't just lead, you'll lead with purpose, with presence, and with impact.

A Personal Note

My journey began with a bike and a bag of newspapers. That paper route taught me what responsibility felt like long before I understood what leadership was. From washing dishes in a small-town restaurant to sitting in executive leadership meetings, every job, every team, every pivot, and every failure has shaped who I am, and who I continue to become. None of it was wasted. Each moment taught me something about work, about people, and most importantly, about myself.

I didn't write this book because I have all the answers, I wrote it because I've been through enough to know what questions to ask. If anything in these pages has made your leadership journey clearer, more intentional, or a little easier to navigate, then writing it was worth every word.

To those who have walked this journey with me, friends, peers, mentors, and even challengers, thank you. Truly thank you. You helped me grow, and in many cases, you believed in me before I believed in myself. And to anyone reading this now, enjoy the ride. Take the work seriously, but not yourself. Stay curious, stay committed, and don't forget to laugh along the way. Leadership can be hard. But it's worth it. And so are you.

This book is dedicated to the countless people on the ladder of success. Regardless of where you are, you're on it, keep climbing until you get to where you want to climb to. I learned invaluable experiences from you, and I hope to return some of those here to others.

www.ingramcontent.com/pod-product-compliance
Lightning Source LLC
Chambersburg PA
CBHW070942210326
41520CB00021B/7012